40 FOUNDATIONS OF FAITH

A Guide Through Your Scriptural Journey

Steven James Siroky

2024
LIBERATION ENTERPRISES, LLC

ISBN 978-1-965326-00-8

Cover design by: Author
Library of Congress Control Number 2018675909
Printed in the United States of America

In the authority and blood of Jesus, I anoint this book and all who read it to break the
bondage of evil and journey in freedom.

Dedication

This is dedicated to my beloved wife of 30+ years, Susan. She is my partner, supporter, encourager, and the one who listens to everything.

I thank my dear friends, Nellie Amedee, Jim Langdal, and the late Otto Lacayo. They helped organize and clarify the 40 Foundations of Faith©.

And thank you to my friends over the years, David Hewitt, Sean Rice, Kurt Stromberg, Mark Miller, Dan Goddard, and Steven Meisenheimer. They have listened to, debated, and discussed many of the concepts within these pages.

And thank you to Mark Buehring and Alice Miller, my prayer warriors, and the others who were part of the early development of Jubilee Days, all listed at thejubileedays.com.

Proceeds from this book will benefit Jubilee Days and other affiliated ministries.

Contents

Preface

This is a bible study, not a devotional. The few scriptural quotations within are all from the King James Bible.

Any study of The Scripture can be challenging. Being prepared for a challenge is an important step in completing it. "How to Use This Study" has important information and guidelines to help you prepare. Please do not skip this step.

The beginning and end of the study include some highlights of my testimony and faith journey. I trust this study and my testimony will assist you in turning belief into a firm foundation of faith.

The Start

It is 2:37 AM on December 20, 2023, and I am starting a book that His Spirit has been asking me to write for over three years. I have avoided writing for all the wrong reasons, mainly relying on my own understanding, but I am starting for the right one. My King, my Savior, my Deliverer, has asked me to.

Throughout my life, His Spirit has pursued me. From my early years in the cornfields of Indiana until now in the deserts of Arizona. I can recall many times when He protected me and when He tested me. I have been both rebellious and faithful, and everything in between. I have been lost and found. I have been in seasons of cold toward Him, seasons of lukewarm, and gratefully many seasons of fire for Him.

In 2002, I realized I was lost and leading my wife to the same end. I came back to Him and became involved with a Christian retreat, Via de Cristo. Since then, he has opened my heart and made it bigger. I find it sometimes overwhelming. Once, I was in a crowd of brothers and sisters singing, "Here I am Lord." I remember distinctly, He asked me to hold all His people in my heart. I said I would. I did back then and still do now. That commitment to my wife, Susan, and to Jesus is at the root of all that I have written.

This study and these pages resulted from the collaboration of very close, dear friends, and my beloved wife, Susan. His Spirit has guided me to add further clarifications to the original study of the 40 Foundations of Faith© making it suitable as a standalone book. I have also included key parts of my personal testimony after the study. I trust I am listening to His Spirit.

The 40 Foundations of Faith© (40 FoF) are the teaching points within Jubilee Days. A Jubilee Days event is several short days designed to experience the principles of life as a Believer and Follower of Jesus through testimonies. The format of the 40 FoF and follow-up questions have been modified for this study.

Because of decisions made by the early Christian leaders, we are taught passages of The Scripture in weekly "bites" by topic or by book. In my experience, the entirety of The Scripture is rarely taught in continuity. The 40 Foundations of Faith© overcome this by collecting key information throughout both Testaments in a systematic process. The format will clarify the basics and likely remove the common misunderstandings of Jesus's Believers and Followers and non-believers.

The 40 Foundations of Faith© study differs from most. It is not meant to convince you of a particular belief, but to guide you into studying the questions and concepts that are fundamental to understanding your faith and your relationship with Jesus.

We hear and see all around us through the filter of what we believe to be true. For example, when I was younger, I did not understand the need for oil in a car engine. I thought a car only needed gasoline to move. I didn't comprehend how the engine or transmission actually worked. I believed, if I just kept the gas tank more than empty, the car engine would still operate, and I would continue to go where I needed. This was true until I had evidence to the contrary.

I drove that car for so long with low oil, the engine seized up. I quickly learned the purpose of oil and how important it is. The engine had specific operations and rules that I did not know or even understand. However, this didn't stop me from driving. We live each day the same way. We live within multiple systems, natural, legal, and governmental, to list a few. These all have their rules and operations around us.

The spiritual system is the same. When we read scripture, we read it with the bias of our current beliefs. Jesus shares a parable about the oil in our lamps.

Matthew 25:1-5

"Then shall the kingdom of heaven be likened unto ten virgins, which took their lamps, and went forth to meet the bridegroom. And five of them were wise, and five were foolish.

They that were foolish took their lamps, and took no oil with them: But the wise took oil in their vessels with their lamps. While the bridegroom tarried, they all slumbered and slept."

What does oil in the lamp mean?

Your mind instantly wants to answer the question with the knowledge you have. This is how we think. We want to answer the question with what we know or think we know. If we do not fully think it through, we can misunderstand it.

Until I knew the purpose of oil in an automobile engine, I misunderstood it or ignored it. Until I understood more of the spiritual reality, I misunderstood it or ignored it. Until I understood that I have had an adversary my entire life, I dismissed it. I do no longer.

The deepest and darkest spiritual reality is that Lucifer hates us. He wishes to destroy humans. If you are trying to live your life with Jesus, he will try to limit your connection to and your influence for The Creator God. In what I have seen, two of Lucifer's greatest weapons are misunderstanding and ignorance. I have grown up in culture discouraged from believing in or studying the truth within scripture.

Although Lucifer possesses knowledge of the ages, he lacks the power of Jesus within us. We don't have to run away from this. We can walk in victory over his world systems with His Spirit. The human "race" is not about sprinting toward wealth, power, excitement, comfort, recreation, or security. These are all distractions.

Paul refers to the real "race" of our faith journey as continually moving forward, comparable to a "marathon," against the influences of The Enemy. This is against our spiritual enemies, those men and women purposely or ignorantly working with them, and all other things of life not directing us to Jesus.

John 14:6 states:

"Jesus saith unto him, I am the way, the truth, and the life: no man cometh unto the Father, but by me."

He is the actual race, persevering to live His **Way**, seek His **Truth**, and find His dynamic **Life** within you.

Why 40?

The Creator God uses specific numbers throughout scripture. There are many examples of sevens. There are: the six days of creation and the seventh day of rest and the six pieces of His Spiritual Armor and the seventh of praying in the spirit. There are many more sevens listed just in John's book of The Revelation. Besides the number seven, there are many references to the numbers 3, 4, 12, and 40.

The number 40 has been referenced primarily for a new start. Below are many of the scriptural examples of 40. They show the order and purpose of The One True God. The more you study scripture, the more these connections occur.

The following are most of the scriptures highlighting 40:

1. The earth experienced the Flood for 40 days and nights of rain. - Genesis 7

2. The Hebrews prepared Jacob's (Israel's) body for 40 days before they mourned or traveled to bury him. - Genisis 50

3. Moses was 40 years old when he rebelled against the Egyptians. - Acts 7

4. After Egypt, Moses lived in Midian 40 years before YHWH came to him as a burning bush. - in Acts 7

5. Moses received The One True God's instructions for 40 days and nights with no food or water on the mountain. - Exodus 24 - 34 and Deuteronomy 9 & 10

6. Joshua was 40 years old when he volunteered to spy on Canan. - Joshua 14

7. Joshua and the other eleven (11) spies searched Canan for 40 days. - Numbers 13

8. YWHW cleansed and showed grace to the Hebrew nation for 40 years with manna and other supernatural provisions. - Exodus 16, Numbers 14, Deuteronomy 2, Nehemiah 9, Psalm 95, Amos 2 & 5, Acts 7 & 13, and Hebrews 3

9. The Law limited the lashings of a wicked man to 40 stripes. - Deuteronomy 25 and 2 Colossians 11

10. After the Hebrews worshipped other gods, The One True God allowed them to be slaves for 40 years three different times. The land rested each of those 40 years. - Judges 3, 5 & 8

11. As punishment, the Philistines enslaved the Hebrews for 40 years. - Judges 13

12. Goliath, the Philistine giant, challenged the army of Israel for a champion for 40 mornings and evenings. - 1 Samuel 17

13. King David reigned for 40 years. - 2 Samuel 5 & 15 and 1 Kings 2

14. The Temple was built to 40 cubits in length (40 x 46 cm or 40 x 18 inches). - 1 Kings 6

15. The Temple basins, washing lavers, held 40 baths (40 x 36 liters or 40 x 9 gallons) in volume. - 1 Kings 7

16. King Solomon reigned for 40 years. - 1 Kings 11, 1 Chronicles 29, and 2 Chronicles 9

17. Elijah had no food or drink for 40 days on Mount Horeb. - Kings 19

18. Hazael offered 40 camels loaded with the good things of Damascus to Elisha. - 2 Kings

19. King Joash reigned for 40 years. - 2 Kings 12 and 2 Chronicles 24

20. Prior to Nehemiah, the former governor levied a tax of 40 shekels of silver (40 x 9.5 grams or 40 x 1/3 ounce) in weight. - Nehemiah 5

21. Ezekial was instructed to lie on his side for 40 days for Judah's inequity. - Ezekial 4

22. As punishment for enslaving the Hebrews, Egypt's lands were desolate for 40 years. - Ezekial 29

23. Nineveh had 40 days to repent before destruction. - Jonah 3

24. Jesus fasted from food for 40 days while being tempted by The Satan. - Matthew 4, Mark 13, and Luke 4

25. Jesus was seen and spoke to people for 40 days after His resurrection. - Acts 1

When reviewing this list, it is evident that there is a supernatural significance in the number 40.

The One True God uses it in various ways at different times. When discerning the heart of these examples, you will find the fundamental reasons are beyond just a new start. He uses 40 for **Repentance, Restoration, and Preparation.** This is why there are 40 Foundations of Faith©. And this is why you should commit to no less than a forty-day study.

How to use this Study

How should anyone best use these 40 Foundations of Faith© (40 FoF)? The 40 FoF were designed to be both shared within the Jubilee Days event and used as a 40-day follow-up study as an individual or with a small group of trusted people.

If you are an individual, commit to take 40 days in a row. If you are a smaller group, commit to the 40 days and meet for six weeks to review only the Deeper Questions. If you are a larger group, you may want to commit to 40 weeks. His Spirit works in all ways, always. No matter what you choose, keep the commitment. There is power in the fulfilling the commitment to Him and studying His word.

Keeping commitments to yourself and others fosters inner strength. This inner strength improves or edifies the temple that you are. Understand that you are the temple of His Spirit.

Paul stated in 1 Corinthians 3:16:

"Know ye not that ye are the temple of God, and that the Spirit of God dwelleth in you?"

You are the temple of His Spirit. In that way, you are like a house with a foundation, walls, and roof. Consider that these 40 Foundations of Faith© are the building blocks to support your house.

The 40 FoF are like concrete blocks in a foundation. They are placed row by row, wall by wall, up to the final height. Your understanding of these foundations may be complete or just beginning. Consequently, through this study, you may need to only strengthen or build in certain areas more than others. I strongly suggest, like a building, you to focus on one wall at a time.

Organization

The study is divided into six groups. These correspond to the six days of a Jubilee Days event. Each group is organized to better understand the subsequent section(s). Each group has a particular theme, key concepts, and a parallel piece of Spiritual Armor.

The groups are:

1. AWARENESS
   This is Real
   Girdle of Truth

2. DESIRE
   The Creator God & Lucifer Both Want Us
   Breastplate of Righteousness

3. RESPONSE
   We Must Choose
   Helmet of Salvation

4. FAITH
   Trust & Act
   Shield of Faith

5. JOURNEY
   Have a Living Relationship
   Shoes of the Gospel

6. COMMITMENT
   Accept Jesus, then Share Him
   Sword of The Spirit and Prayer in The Spirit

If you look at this study as building your spiritual foundation, the groups can be understood, as illustrated below.

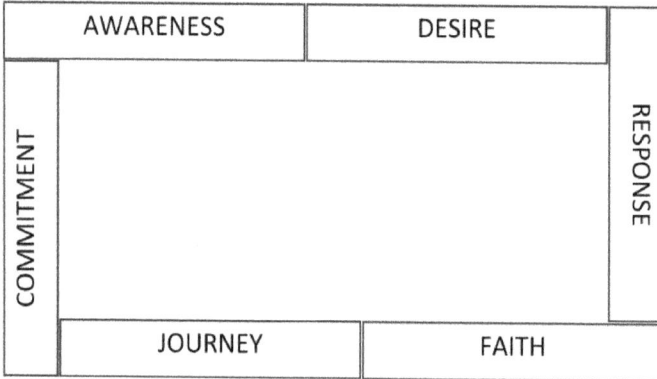

	AWARENESS	DESIRE	
COMMITMENT			RESPONSE
	JOURNEY	FAITH	

Group 1 & Group 2 pair to make up the primary long wall, neighboring Group 3, a shorter wall, followed by Group 4 & Group 5, the additional long wall, and completing the rectangle with Group 6, the other short wall.

Each of the six groups has several of The 40 Foundations of Faith© lessons. Group order matters more than lesson order. Group 1 should be studied in its entirety before proceeding to Group 2, and so on.

Each FoF starts with an introduction to the concepts. Then has key study points, scriptural examples, and follow-up questions. The FoF detailed in the upcoming chapters are:

AWARENESS
1. TRUTH
2. IMAGE
3. FATHER
4. RANSOM
5. YEARNING
6. CONVERSATION

DESIRE
7. ENEMY
8. DECEIVED
9. PROPHESIED
10. GRACE
11. LOVE
12. BOND
13. INHERITANCE

RESPONSE
14. REBORN
15. PLANTED
16. UNDERSTANDING
17. IMPORTANCE
18. PLEDGE
19. JOY
20. SERVED

FAITH
  21. COMPASSION
  22. TRUST
  23. OUTREACH
  24. EMPOWERED
  25. FREEDOM
  26. FIERCE
  27. HUNGER

JOURNEY
  28. WRESTLING
  29. CONNECTED
  30. PROTECTED
  31. COUNSEL
  32. SUPPORT
  33. HOME

COMMITMENT
  34. BLESSED
  35. CONTINUE
  36. ABUNDANCE
  37. PURPOSE
  38. PARTNERSHIP
  39. COMFORT
  40. COMMIT

Terminology

You will notice throughout this book the absence of common Christian names and terms. Our American English uses the same word to mean several different ideas. Likewise, many religious systems use the same generic terms as Christians, such as God, Anointed, or Messiah. Our spiritual enemies use these same terms to confuse or deceive us. Because of this, Christians will use the generic terms to avoid offending or confronting other people.

The terms used are:

The One True God, The Godhead, The Creator God, or YHWH are used instead of God or Lord. God or Lord are used by many other religious systems.

Jesus is used instead of Christ, Anointed or Messiah. These, like God or Lord, are used by many other religious systems.

His Spirit is used instead of Holy Ghost, Holy Spirit, or The Spirit. These three choices for The One True God's Spirit are used by many other religious systems. There are billions or even trillions of spirits, but only His Spirit will guide you to Truth and to Jesus.

The Scripture or His Word are used instead of the Bible. Scripture is the inspired Word of The One True God. There are numerous versions and translations of the Bible. Some of them will have 66, 73, 81, up to 88 books. There are Bibles purposely changed to hide various key facts. Trust His Spirit will guide you into all truth.

Jesus's Believers and Followers is used instead of Christians. A Believer and Follower is a person with an active relationship with Jesus. They believe in their mind and in their heart in the full truth of Jesus and actively demonstrate that belief as a living testimony. In our current cultures, many call themselves Christian because they were raised in Christian home, or go to worship services, or participate in Christian activities, or have said the "sinners prayer" in their life. Although these may be true for a person who is in active relationship with Jesus, it does not make the relationship true. A true Christian both believes and follows Jesus.

Religious System is used instead of Faith, Church, or Religion.

Lucifer or The Satan are used instead of Helel, Devil, Adversary, or Satan. All of these names are characteristics of his part in our lives. Any spirit can play these roles: Helel or Lucifer means "light bearer" or knowledge giver and inspiration, Devil means mischief and trickery, Adversary means opposition, and Satan means accuser. There is only one, Lucifer, The Satan, the cast out arch angel, with sin found in him who rebelled against The One True God.

The Enemy is used to include Lucifer and all that he controls. This includes both demonic entities, other heavenly hosts, and all the human men and women purposely serving them.

Preparing for the Study

Before starting this study, prayerfully seek His guidance and ask these questions.

- Should I include a fast as part of this study?

- What do I want to learn about myself and you?

- What do I need to change about myself?

These answers will help personalize your journey and ensure you are aligned with His plan.

When choosing which scripture translation to read, I suggest you read the King James or Geneva. Although they are not perfect and use language that can be challenging, they have the closest translation to the "Received Text" or original manuscripts.

If their language becomes challenging, I suggest that you read another translation in addition to those for comparison. You will find areas where the translations differ. These variations may offer you clarity to the words used. Additionally, with online translations, you can easily refer to the Greek or Hebrew.

When reading scripture, there are a few simple guidelines to remember:

1. These words were written to those living in the past with a different culture, different understandings, and different lifestyle than us.

2. The Hebrew culture commonly did not write events chronologically. Instead, they would start with a topic summary, then go into further detail, like a typical news article.

3. An overwhelming number of the books were written as a recount of history, by many different authors. It is not a fictional story to illustrate ideas. There are writings that are poetry and parables, but those are a small percentage.

4. If words or ideas you are reading seem confusing, then read the original Hebrew or Greek translations. Our current translations of these languages will use the same word to convey a variety of subtle differences.

5. Most importantly, scripture is spiritual. The Enemy does not want you to read it. However, His Spirit does. Sincerely, ask The One True God to guide you and teach you what He wants you to understand.

We are created with souls, which are the source of our gift of emotions. When reading scripture or when in prayer, you may experience emotions, positive and negative. Unfortunately, our negative emotions can impede understanding and logic much more than positive emotions.

These typically occur when learning information contrary to our current beliefs. This is referred to as "cognitive dissonance" in psychology. It is the term to describe the mental and physical discomfort or stress we experience when we see, experience, or start to believe a truth contrary to our current beliefs.

From my personal experience, to change your beliefs is painful, both physically and emotionally. As I understood more of scripture, I discovered truths I had to reconcile or integrate with my existing beliefs. These were painful. It felt like I was grieving. Instead of a loved one dying, I experienced the loss and death of myself and my identity.

Being confronted with a change in your beliefs will cause you to wrestle with yourself. These changes may lead you to question the motives of friends and family. You may question your previous decisions on entertainment, career, location to live. You may question your ideal way of life. After you decide to change, next you will grieve all of these. But once these struggles are over and the grief ends, you will stand firmer in your beliefs and stronger in your faith.

Our human souls do not like to be told we are wrong. When you share these different beliefs with others, you might be "put down" as stupid or deceived or just receive their anger. This is their cognitive dissonance reacting to what you are sharing, by word or action. They experience the same pain as you did, but now they project it onto you.

As noted earlier with the terminology, one of The Enemy's strategies is deceiving. This can occur as distorting or hiding essential information. The Enemy has purposely attacked the validity of scripture.

Faith is not just believing, it is knowing. His Spirit will let you know when something is personally important, and if now is the right time to study it.

If you are not a believer or you are questioning your belief, I suggest, commit to the next 40 days or so and read through a new Foundation of Faith each day. Take as much time as you can. This will create within you a more complete grasp of the knowledge and information. If you skip around, you may not develop a full understanding.

In a study like this, for whatever reason, emotions will arise. Please take the time to let emotions pass and then refocus on the topic. If you feel emotionally "stuck," write that down or mark the key point or scripture causing it and return to it later.

If you are feeling "bogged down" or overwhelmed, do not dwell on any one day too long. Keep the same amount of time committed daily. Taking 10 - 15 minutes a day is enough to read the information and a scriptural example or two. While 20 - 30 minutes a day would give you time to journal or answer some of the questions.

The discipline of study is a commitment to yourself. It is a lifelong marathon, not a sprint. Many times, understanding can only occur after other events or knowledge is fully understood. This was proven throughout much of the development of this study. His Spirit would lead us to an idea or key fact with the note that this would be explained later. This is His way, always preparing you for something new.

The scriptures are living words. They are empowered by His Spirit to you personally. It is not a fictional story; it is a letter from The Creator God through the lives of people in our past. The scriptures have depth and meaning throughout your entire life. A passage read weeks or months later will have a different or deeper meaning, depending on your current circumstances.

Take the time you need through this study. Prepare mentally, emotionally, and spiritually for each day of study. Go through the study as many times as you want. It is designed for all levels of understanding. Paul (Saul) told Timothy in 2 Timothy 2:15:

"Study to shew thyself approved unto God, a workman that needeth not to be ashamed, rightly dividing the word of truth."

I pray that these days of study will become as fulfilling and powerful for you as they have been for me and those who helped develop them.

AWARENESS - *This is Real*

Learn the Truth of Jesus and remove the lies you believe from your mind.

This is the first group of Foundations of Faith. It is likely the biggest challenge for non-believers and those struggling with The One True God or Jesus. The debate of the accuracy and authenticity of scripture is the first battlefield of The Enemy. The proof of its accuracy is within its own pages.

Here are the basic understandings for this group. They will be explored deeper in FoF #01 - #06:

The Scriptures are true.

The One True God created every human being.

Lucifer sinned first and holds humanity captive.

Understanding the Truth frees us to be with The Godhead, Creator again.

Gird Your Waist with TRUTH

Ephesians 6:14 "...your loins girt about with truth..."

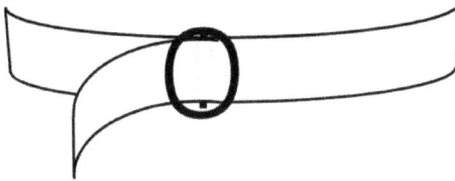

FoF #01 – TRUTH

Scriptures are the real Inspired Words of The One True God, supported by archeological, historical, and manuscript evidence.

We see creation around us every day, either made by man or by The One True God. If you doubt the truth of scripture, then this is a key FoF for you. There is significant evidence that supports scripture as His Word. His Word is so important He had Ptolemy of Egypt around 200 BC had Hebrew scholars translate the numerous books of the Old Testament into Greek. Ensuring that the people were ready for His Son.

If your mind does not want to believe it, then stop the study and seek the evidence highlighted below before continuing. The greatest challenge within this age of information is knowing what you can trust. His Spirit inspired different people to write these words to direct you to Him.

The One True God offers us real freedom in His relationship. Read, study, and discern His Word for your life.

Key points of FoF #01:

1. **The entirety of Scripture is inspired by His Spirit.**

2. **It must be read in context by the book, not just by chapter and verse. It was written for the people of that time, but applicable to us.**

3. **The Septuagint (LXX) was written in common Greek by the highest Hebrew scholars hundreds of years before Jesus was born.**

4. **The evidence supporting the accuracy of the New Testament is over abundant. There are 24,000+ manuscript documents all written within 100 years of Jesus's life.**

5. **Scripture contains over 700 fulfilled prophesies.**

Here are the scriptural examples of FoF #01:

- 2 Timothy 3:16-17
- Matthew 7:24-29
- 1 Corinthians 13:4-6
- Isaiah 46:8-11
- Proverbs 30:4-6
- Hebrews 4:12-13
- Romans 1:18-23
- Hosea 4:6
- Isaiah 28:9-13
- Proverbs 15:29
- Matthew 24:3-5
- Proverbs 25:2
- Psalm 104

Individual or Group Discussion Questions:

1. What concept or fact above made you think the most?

2. What person in the scriptural examples did you connect with the most?

3. What emotions were stirred within you? What is the source of that emotion?

FoF #02 – IMAGE

All people are made to be The Creator's representatives on Earth.

All creatures were created by The One True God. We see some of them roaming, flying, or swimming about the earth. Some of them we do not see, such as microorganisms and the spiritual beings. When He created us as a species, He made us similar to Him and gave us dominion and position within His hierarchy. If you believe you are not worthy of His love and attention, then you do not understand Him and His relationship with you.

Know this: you were created by Him with the "spark of life." You were not created by accident. Your existence was not just from a physical act of a man and woman or a sperm and egg, but a divine act. Take the time to study reproductive biology. You will see that the conception of humans is a miracle. You are a miracle. You are here on earth, reading this book, because He wants to have a relationship with you and give you the gift of importance.

Key points of FoF #02:

1. **The One True God is three in one: The Father/Creator, The Son/Jesus, & The Holy/His Spirit.**

2. **We are primarily three: Soul, Body, and Spirit.**

3. **We were created in His image to live with Him in a perfect relationship and through His authority.**

4. **We are princes or princesses in God's inner court. We were to rule on Earth.**

Here are the scriptural examples of FoF #02:

- Genesis 1:26-31
- Psalm 8:1-9
- Genesis 2:15-24
- Matthew 10:29-31
- Luke 12:6-7
- Jeremiah 1:4-5
- John 1:1-5
- Psalm 139:1-18

Individual or Group Discussion Questions:

1. What concept or fact above made you think the most?

2. What person in the scriptural examples did you connect with the most?

3. What emotions were stirred within you? What is the source of that emotion?

FoF #03 – FATHER

The One True God yearns for a covenant relationship with us, just like Adam and Eve.

When we humans were first made, we were given a special home filled with everything we would need and given the earth to reign over and manage. At that time, we were intimate with all creatures and The One True God. We had conversations with Him regularly. We walked with Him.

It was perfection, but Lucifer rebelled and led us to rebel with him. From the time of our exile from Eden, we have had sin in us and on the Earth. And in His perfect love, He wants us to return to that deeply intimate relationship with Him.

Key points of FoF #03:

1. Lucifer tempted Adam and Eve to be like The One True God. They chose to disobey and ate the fruit of Knowledge of Good and Evil.

2. Humankind was spiritually separated from the Creator God because of their disobedience. Because of this sin, every person is born under The Satan's reign.

3. The Creator God yearns for a renewed relationship with us.

4. The One True God gives us the choice to change from being under The Satan's reign to be under His.

Here are the scriptural examples of FoF #03:

- John 3:10-21
- Psalm 95:1-10
- Psalm 139:1-18
- Song of Solomon 4:7-11
- Genesis 3:8-9

Individual or Group Discussion Questions:

1. What concept or fact above made you think the most?

2. What person in the scriptural examples did you connect with the most?

3. What emotions were stirred within you? What is the source of that emotion?

FoF #04 – RANSOM

Mankind's sin required a perfect sacrifice. Jesus fulfilled that and enabled us to change.

Because of Adam's disobedience, our human existence has had sin in it. This "original" sin allowed in the curse that took over the perfection of the earth, us, and other creatures. Mankind's first sin was disobedience. This separated us from the perfect relationship with Creator God.

His law requires a blood sacrifice or death to pay for sin. We sin today, when we disobey His Word or His guidance in our lives. Jesus was that sacrifice for mankind's sin as well as our own sin today.

Key points of FoF #04:

1. **Jesus's death was payment for our sin.**

2. **This payment is offered to all people.**

3. **It is my choice to receive this gift of grace.**

Here are the scriptural examples of FoF #04:

- John 17:1-5
- John 1:6-34
- 1 Peter 2:21-25
- Romans 5:6-19

Individual or Group Discussion Questions:

1. What concept or fact above made you think the most?

2. What person in the scriptural examples did you connect with the most?

3. What emotions were stirred within you? What is the source of that emotion?

FoF #05 — YEARNING

Our hearts are made to connect with Him.

The Godhead created our hearts to be in a perfectly intimate relationship with Him. Without Him, our hearts crave that missing intimacy and desires it from things around us. Our body houses the heart or inner man. The heart is a generic term to include all the non-physical parts of us inside.

Our body's five senses transmit our experience and environment to our heart/inner man. The heart has three parts with four descriptions: mind, conscience, and the soul, which has the will and emotion. Our spiritual body, the innermost man, connects to our outer body through the heart.

This connection was perfect until the curse damaged it and allowed our sin to impede that connection. Our hearts yearn to have that perfect connection with The Creator God established again.

Key points of FoF #05:

1. **We were intimately created by Him.**

2. **We connect to Him through our heart/inner man. Without Him, our heart/inner man still craves that relationship.**

3. **Our five senses receive from the world around us, and our mind and emotions processes it. Our spirit through the conscience and will respond back.**

4. **Sin affects our mind and emotions, and over time, it can affect our will and conscience.**

5. **In the end with The Creator God, we can return to the perfection we were.**

Here are the scriptural examples of FoF #05:

- 1 Corinthians 2:10-16
- Ezekiel 36:24-28
- Psalm 63:1-5
- Romans 7
- Job 10
- Deuteronomy 6:4-6
- Titus 1:10-16
- Hebrews 8:7-12
- Romans 12:1-2
- 1 Timothy 4:1-5
- 1 Peter 3:13-22
- 1 Peter 2:7-12
- Exodus 8:5-15

Individual or Group Discussion Questions:

1. What concept or fact above made you think the most?

2. What person in the scriptural examples did you connect with the most?

3. What emotions were stirred within you? What is the source of that emotion?

FoF #06 – CONVERSATION

You must separate yourself from the worldly distractions or "noise" and make time to hear Him clearly.

To understand and hear The Creator God clearly, you must give Him time and attention. Just like a friendship or marriage, communication is essential. In today's culture and busy lifestyle, we either lack the time or desire to do so. We are distracted by information and entertainment through the technology of phones, computers, radio, and television.

He is not just a power source you can plug into for improvements in our lives. But a true Father, that cares and understands us better than we can imagine. He desires a deep and meaningful relationship with us. Listen, speak, ask questions, and wait for answers.

Key points of FoF #06:

1. Conversation and communication are necessary for our relationship with The One True God.

2. This requires active listening, thinking, seeking, and questioning.

3. Scripture can be understood as "The Living Word" or a "Love Letter" and can be used as part of prayer and active listening.

4. Prayer and/or conversation with The Creator God can occur in many ways, including worship and praise.

Here are the scriptural examples of FoF #06:

- Isaiah 26:8-9
- Psalm 46:7-11
- 1 Thessalonians 5:17-23
- Joshua 1:8
- Psalm 119:9-11
- Matthew 6:5-8
- Isaiah 26:3
- 2 Corinthians 4:1-4
- Psalm 84

Individual or Group Discussion Questions:

1. What concept or fact above made you think the most?

2. What person in the scriptural examples did you connect with the most?

3. What emotions were stirred within you? What is the source of that emotion?

4. *** SPECIAL Homework - What steps will you take to prioritize your relationship with Him?**

Group 1 – AWARENESS: *Deeper Questions*

The Deeper Questions below are meant for an in-depth study of this group. These questions can be completed any time after finishing Group 1 - AWARENESS.

1. Which of these basic understandings has a new meaning to you or resonated with you?

   ➢ The Scriptures are true.
   ➢ The One True God created every human being.
   ➢ Lucifer sinned first and holds humanity captive.
   ➢ Understanding the Truth frees us to be with The Godhead, Creator again.

2. Which Foundation of Faith was most significant to you?

   FoF #01 – TRUTH
   FoF #02 – IMAGE
   FoF #03 – FATHER
   FoF #04 – RANSOM
   FoF #05 – YEARNING
   FoF #06 – CONVERSATION

3. What in this Foundation of Faith made it so significant?

4. In that significant Foundation of Faith, read at least one more Scriptural Example. Did this improve your understanding of it?

5. Why is **Truth** part of His Spiritual Armor for us?

6. How does your understanding of The One True God differ after studying Group 1 -AWARNESS?

7. How will your relationships with other people change?

DESIRE – *The Creator God & Lucifer Both Want Us*

With Jesus, your Heart is protected.

This is the second group of Foundations of Faith. This group refers to the current state of our spiritual life. Understand this, His love for us is so great, that He gave us dominion of the earth. It is truly a battlefield for our worship and, ultimately, our eternal life.

Because of sin and the curse, we are physically separated from the perfect relationship with The Creator God. In that separation, we are exposed to the temptations and obstacles of The Enemy. However, this is not final. He has made the way to get back.

Here are the basic understandings for this group. They will be explored deeper in FoF #07 - #13:

Jesus desires for us to be one with Him forever.

Lucifer desires to replace The Creator God.

The Satan and his followers aggressively manipulate us with our worldly desires.

Jesus wants us so much, he died to redeem us, releasing us from The Satan's power.

Secure the Breastplate of RIGHTOUSNESS

Ephesians 6:16 "…and having on the breastplate of righteousness;"

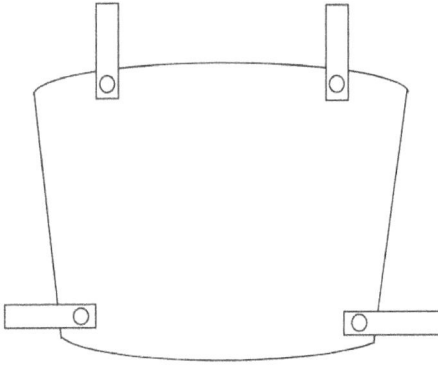

FoF #07 – ENEMY

Lucifer, The Satan, rebelled and hates you and me.

Lucifer rebelled against The One True God coveting what He had, His as sovereign rule of everything, and our authority on the Earth through Jesus. Lucifer became the adversary to all people and especially anyone who could stand with The One True God.

From the moment your life began, you had an opponent who you did not see or understand. Lucifer uses his power over people and natural systems to keep our focus elsewhere. Lucifer will do anything to anyone to distract us from The One True God.

Key points of FoF #07:

1. **Before we were made, Lucifer was the highest level of created heavenly being, an archangel, in whom sin began.**

2. **When we were created, we were made to be in authority on Earth and shared a special relationship with The Creator.**

3. **Lucifer wants to be The One True God.**

4. **Lucifer and his army operate on earth and in the atmosphere continually working against us.**

Here are the scriptural examples of FoF #07:

- Matthew 24:9-13
- Matthew 4:1-9
- John 8:37-44
- Isaiah 14:12-14
- The Revelation 12:7-17
- Luke 10:17-20
- 1 Corinthians 15:33-45
- Colossians 1:16-17
- Ephesians 1:21-22
- Romans 8:38-39
- Job 1 & 2
- Colossians 2:13-15
- Ephesians 3:9-12
- Ephesians 6:12
- The Revelation 20

Individual or Group Discussion Questions:

1. What concept or fact above made you think the most?

2. What person in the scriptural examples did you connect with the most?

3. What emotions were stirred within you? What is the source of that emotion?

FoF #08 – DECEIVED

Lucifer led us astray; in turn, we gave up our authority and lost the keys to the kingdom.

When Lucifer persuaded Eve, then Eve persuaded Adam to eat of the Tree of Knowledge of Good and Evil, they rebelled and disobeyed The Creator God. This led humans into sin. This separated us from our perfect connection with YWHW.

They were removed from the Garden of Eden and stripped of their highest authority on Earth. Today, we live within the authority of The Enemy, The Satan and his abundant armies continually working against us. For Jesus's Believers and Followers, this changes.

Key points of FoF #08:

1. **Lucifer hated our authority on earth. Then, in the Garden of Eden, he lied and stole it.**

2. **Jesus explained The Satan's intent is to lie, steal and murder.**

3. **Since his defeat by Jesus, The Satan continues trying to keep us from receiving The One True God's authority and power of His Spirit.**

Here are the scriptural examples of FoF #08:

- Matthew 10:16-24
- Genesis 3:17-24
- 2 Corinthians 11:13-14
- 1 Timothy 4:1-6
- 1 Samuel 15:13-24
- 1 John 4:1-6
- John 8:33-47
- Acts 4:24-26
- Psalm 2
- The Revelation 12:7-9
- The Revelation 16:13-16
- The Revelation 20:1-10

Individual or Group Discussion Questions:

1. What concept or fact above made you think the most?

2. What person in the scriptural examples did you connect with the most?

3. What emotions were stirred within you? What is the source of that emotion?

FoF #09 – PROPHESIED

Jesus fulfilled all the laws and many prophesies.

Prophecy is one of the key proofs that Scripture is real and accurate. Jesus is noted in over 300 direct and indirect prophecies and references. If you calculated the odds of one man fulfilling the basic 15 prophecies, they are approximately 1 in 1 with 72 zeros ($1/10^{72}$). The odds of being struck by lightning are 1 in 1 with 6 zeros ($1/10^{6}$).

His existence, birth, life, death, resurrection, current location were each foretold directly and indirectly throughout the old testament. Even the shape of a cross is the old Hebrew shape of the letter "Tah." The letter meant "mark," "sign," or "covenant." It was seen in the formation of the Hebrew camp after leaving Egypt. And a cross of wood was how the Passover lamb was prepared.

Key points of FoF #09:

1. **Jesus' life, crucifixion, death, and resurrection fulfilled over 30 explicit prophecies in the Old Testament.**

2. **His sacrifice is the lamb killed at Passover.**

3. **A cross is the letter Tah, in older Hebrew. It means "sign" or "covenant" and is referenced throughout Scripture as a symbol of Jesus.**

Here are the scriptural examples of FoF #09:

- Luke 4:14-24
- Isaiah 40:1-5
- Matthew 5:17-20
- Acts 3:17-26
- Luke 18:31-33
- 1 Corinthians 15:3-10
- Isaiah 53
- Zechariah 9:9-10
- Micah 7:19-20
- Zechariah 9:9
- Ezekial 11:19-20
- Psalm 22
- Isaiah 7
- The Revelation 1:8-11
- The Revelation 22:12-13

Individual or Group Discussion Questions:

1. What concept or fact above made you think the most?

2. What person in the scriptural examples did you connect with the most?

3. What emotions were stirred within you? What is the source of that emotion?

FoF #10 – GRACE

Jesus is the Godhead, and His Grace is free for all.

From that moment in the Garden of Eden, The Creator God confirmed that death was required for our sin. Initially, it was only a temporary covering with the sacrifice of animals. Then it was final payment with Jesus' life and death.

Grace is an expression of the perfect love He has for us. Even through our disobedience and rebellion, He continually beckons for us and guides us back. Grace is His mercy and kindness, making it possible to eliminate our separation from Him. No longer through ritual or animal and food sacrifices, but through His own sacrifice.

Key points of FoF #10:

1. **Grace is the love and power of The Godhead working through heaven and earth to bring people back to Him.**

2. **Grace was expressed in Jesus' sacrifice.**

3. **Grace is for all people.**

Here are the scriptural examples of FoF #10:

- Colossians 2:8-23
- John 1:14-18
- Galatians 1:3-5
- Galatians 2:11-21
- Romans 5:12-19
- Romans 10:1-13
- Jeremiah 31:31-34

Individual or Group Discussion Questions:

1. What concept or fact above made you think the most?

2. What person in the scriptural examples did you connect with the most?

3. What emotions were stirred within you? What is the source of that emotion?

FoF #11 – LOVE

He runs to meet us with open arms and the keys in hand.

Throughout The Scripture, The Creator God demonstrates His desire for a relationship with us. It is described like a Father to His children and a Husband to His wife or betrothed bride. He gives us everything that He has: authority, protection, justice, provision, guidance, life, and purpose.

He wants us to receive these benefits and gifts so much that He does not wait for our full return to Him. If we just turn toward Him and start walking, He will run to meet us where we are.

Key points of FoF #11:

1. **His eternal love is beyond human understanding.**

2. **He will always run to meet us when we repent, returning to Him like the prodigal son.**

3. **He will accept us until the very last minute, like the parable of laborers in the vineyard.**

Here are the scriptural examples of FoF #11:

- Luke 15:11-32
- John 10: 11-18
- Matthew 20:1-16
- Galatians 5:7-15
- Matthew 9:13
- Isaiah 5:1-7
- Luke 20:9-16
- The Revelation 1:17-18

Individual or Group Discussion Questions:

1. What concept or fact above made you think the most?

2. What person in the scriptural examples did you connect with the most?

3. What emotions were stirred within you? What is the source of that emotion?

FoF #12 – BOND

Receiving communion is both the partaking of His sacrifice and accepting the marriage proposal.

The Passover celebration includes four cups of wine. Each is selected at different times throughout the dinner, and each is presented with different a meaning. The fourth is the cup of Fulfillment, which is not drunk in the Passover celebration. This was the cup specifically saved for the time when the Messiah would finally redeem the Hebrews.

When Jesus celebrated His last Passover with the disciples, He took the fourth cup up and said the words used in a traditional Hebrew marriage betrothal. This is the cup that Christians use for communion. He is inviting every one of us to enter a covenant, a legal promise, with Him.

Key points of FoF #12:

1. **Communion is the "Fulfillment" cup of Passover.**

2. **His greatest desire is to have us as His bride. The Institution of Communion is Jesus' wedding proposal to us.**

3. **To enter into the relationship, we must say "Yes" to His proposal.**

Here are the scriptural examples of FoF #12:

- Ephesians 5:22-33
- Isaiah 62:1-5
- Luke 22:17-20
- Hosea 2:16-20
- 1 Corinthians 11:23-34
- Genisis 24

Individual or Group Discussion Questions:

1. What concept or fact above made you think the most?

2. What person in the scriptural examples did you connect with the most?

3. What emotions were stirred within you? What is the source of that emotion?

FoF #13 – INHERITANCE

Through our relationship with Jesus, we inherit all that He has.

By saying "Yes" to Jesus, we, His Believers and Followers, inherit His kingdom as prince/princess from a king, a child from a father, and wife from a husband. We are given the rights to all that He has, including righteousness through His Spirit.

As His prince/princess, we receive all the rights and responsibilities of a royal family. He sees our righteousness through the bloodline. We are expected to still obey and honor the king through our actions.

As His child, He will allow us to use His gifts as we grow and mature with Him. We may find times where we are tested and need to prove our faithfulness. In the end, we will inherit His new earth.

In the ancient Hebrew wedding tradition, there were three stages: the contract, the bride's verification, and the wedding feast. Today, As His wife, we are in stage two waiting for the full inheritance to come at the wedding feast.

Key points of FoF #13:

1. **We have received His Spirit living inside in our bodily temple.**

2. **We have received full royal citizenship and rights to His kingdom, power, and wisdom.**

3. **We have received His righteousness.**

4. **We have the promise of His return and our perfect future home with no curse and resurrected physical bodies.**

Here are the scriptural examples of FoF #13:

- Romans 3:9-26
- Galatians 4:1-7
- John 3:35-36
- Romans 8:12-17
- 1 Peter 1:3-12
- The Revelation 21:1-7
- John 14:2
- John 1:11-13

Individual or Group Discussion Questions:

1. What concept or fact above made you think the most?

2. What person in the scriptural examples did you connect with the most?

3. What emotions were stirred within you? What is the source of that emotion?

Group 2 – DESIRE: *Deeper Questions*

The Deeper Questions below are meant for an in-depth study of this group. These questions can be completed any time after finishing Group 2 – DESIRE.

1. Which of these basic understandings has a new meaning to you or resonated with you?

   ➢ Jesus desires for us to be one with Him forever.
   ➢ Lucifer desires to replace The Creator God.
   ➢ The Satan and his followers aggressively manipulate us with our worldly desires.
   ➢ Jesus wants us so much, he died to redeem us, releasing us from The Satan's power.

2. Which Foundation of Faith was most significant to you?

   FoF #07 – ENEMY
   FoF #08 – DECEIVED
   FoF #09 – PROPHESIED
   FoF #10 – GRACE
   FoF #11 – LOVE
   FoF #12 – BOND
   FoF #13 – INHERITANCE

3. What in this study made it so significant?

4. In that significant Foundation of Faith, read at least one more Scriptural Example. Did this improve your understanding of it?

5. Why is **<u>Righteousness</u>** part of His Spiritual Armor for us?

6. How does your understanding of The One True God differ after studying Group 2 – DESIRE?

7. How will your relationships with other people change?

RESPONSE - *We Must Choose*

Your decisions in life are best made through eternal thinking with Jesus.

This is the third group of Foundations of Faith. You have likely heard the idea that life is a series of choices. Although generally true, we actually only have one choice. We have one eternally important decision: will we follow with Jesus or not? Once you are His, you can see things with an eternal perspective. You will live differently.

He states that narrow is the gate. A shepherd's gate is just big enough for the shepherd and one sheep or one person at a time. We will all come to this gate and stand next to the shepherd. You alone must choose to be His.

Here are the basic understandings for this group. They will be explored deeper in FoF #14 - #20:

A living relationship with Jesus awakens us.

Our willing relationship is the response to His grace and love.

Building our relationship with Jesus requires our active participation.

Our relationship will change us. We will live differently than those in the world.

Strap on the Helmet of SALVATION

Ephesians 6:16 "And take the helmet of salvation, ..."

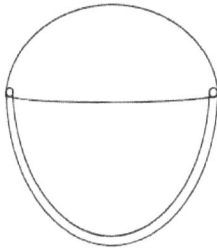

FoF #14 – REBORN

I am born twice and baptized twice, in the body and in the spirit. Then, He washes me daily.

We can experience two births. We receive life and are physically born, then we choose to be spiritually born. Our physical birth began with an inherited curse. The curse spiritually separates us from The One True God. To be born in the spirit or "reborn," we must accept Jesus's gift of salvation, His kingship, and His Spirit within us. His Spirit residing inside of us will be felt or experienced as "coming alive" within.

We can experience two baptisms. We choose a physical baptism, and we receive a spiritual baptism. Our physical water baptism occurs when we obey Him and His word. The physical baptism is our outward indication of our internal commitment to Him. Our spiritual baptism occurs when we fully accept or receive and obey and His Spirit working within us. His Spiritual fruit and gifts are the outward indication of this spiritual baptism.

Once reborn, we no longer need to have the curse removed. We are just required to obey Jesus. He will forgive us of our sins when we confess and repent of them. Jesus exemplified this with the cleansing of His disciples' feet.

Key points of FoF #14:

1. **Through Jesus' death, we can be born again.**

2. **Rebirth is essential for salvation and removes The curse of sin and death.**

3. **Rebirth is a real experience of His Spirit inside of me.**

4. **After Rebirth, only daily washing is needed to remove our worldly sins through confession and repentance.**

Here are the scriptural examples of FoF #14:

- John 3:1-17
- 2 Corinthians 4:1-6
- John 1:10-13
- 1 Peter 1:22-25
- 1 Corinthians 3:16-17
- Romans 8:9-16
- Acts 2:1-4
- Acts 5:29-32
- Acts 19:1-6
- 1 Corinthians 12:1-11
- Matthew 3:7-12
- Mark 1:1-8
- Luke 3:10-17
- Acts 1:1-8
- John 6:32-40

Individual or Group Discussion Questions:

1. What concept or fact above made you think the most?

2. What person in the scriptural examples did you connect with the most?

3. What emotions were stirred within you? What is the source of that emotion?

*SPECIAL Homework -

a) Do you desire to be spiritually born? If yes, this is His Spirit drawing you to Him. Right now, surrender to Jesus and allow His Spirit into you.

b) Do you desire to be physically baptized? This is a beautiful expression of obedience and devotion to Jesus. Jesus desires for you to surrender to His will for your life. A physical baptism declares your internal rebirth externally. This can be done publicly or privately with a pastor, chaplain or other trusted and like-minded counsel.

FoF #15 – PLANTED

When I choose Jesus, I am planted for His purpose and fed with His Truth and Life.

Another analogy of our relationship with The Godhead is we are a plant with Him as our gardener. We should fully rely on Him for provision, protection, and pruning. Our life and our faith journey is directly affected by receiving His work in us and for us. He has placed us in a specific location within His garden. We are where we are for a purpose. Our purpose could be as simple as providing shade and protection for a few or to produce fruit to feed a hundred.

A gardener feeds and waters plants. Likewise, we need His Word as nourishment and His Living Water as refreshment, to survive and thrive on Earth. He will give us what we need when we need it. He will prune us and remove the dead branches, so we grow straight and tall and produce the most fruit as well as provide shade and shelter for others.

Key points of FoF #15:

1. **My connection to the Truth brings me through the things of the world.**

2. **My bond to Jesus' Life strengthens me and feeds my faith.**

3. **My growth is directly because of His work in me.**

Here are the scriptural examples of FoF #15:

- Mark 4:1-9, 13-20
- Luke 3:21-22
- Ephesians 3:14-19
- John 14:19-28
- John 15:1-7
- Psalm 1:1-3
- Luke 13:18-19
- John 4:7-14

Individual or Group Discussion Questions:

1. What concept or fact above made you think the most?

2. What person in the scriptural examples did you connect with the most?

3. What emotions were stirred within you? What is the source of that emotion?

FoF #16 – UNDERSTANDING

My Spiritual heart desires to know Him better.

He created us to need Him. We have a part of our soul that desires a relationship with Him. Our need for Him is spiritually and emotionally similar to other relationships. Like a father to his children, He knows us and wants to guide us and protect us.

Our spirit does not become alive until His lives within us. We must come to The Godhead with a childlike mind, curious, hopeful, and trusting. When this occurs, we are given direct access to The Godhead. Learning His Word and talking directly with Him is the best way to truly know Him.

Key points of FoF #16:

1. **He desires I come to Him with the wonder and open heart of a child.**

2. **He desires I listen and obey Him, so He can protect and bless me.**

3. **His Spirit desires to lead me in understanding the Scriptures.**

4. **His Spirit desires to guide me in my life's situations.**

Here are the scriptural examples of FoF #16:

- Luke 18:15-17
- John 4:19-26
- Ephesians 1:15-21
- Colossians 2:4-10
- Matthew 13:44-45
- Acts 17:10-12
- Psalm 119

Individual or Group Discussion Questions:

1. What concept or fact above made you think the most?

2. What person in the scriptural examples did you connect with the most?

3. What emotions were stirred within you? What is the source of that emotion?

FoF #17 – IMPORTANCE

My relationship and time with Jesus is the greatest priority.

Our relationship with The Creator God is most important to our lives on earth and beyond. He knows you intimately. He knows what is best for you and those important to you. Time spent with Him is crucial in allowing you to hear Him clearly. This is more than just the time needed to study. This includes worship, prayer, and discussions with those around you.

As you spend more time with Him, you will hear Him more clearly. He desires to give you protection, guidance, fulfillment of your true desires, and to help you help others. To receive these gifts, you must spend time with Him.

Key points of FoF #17:

1. **We should want to be in a relationship and loved by Him.**

2. **We should want to spend time in His presence at His feet, listening.**

3. **Jesus knows and guides me to my heart's true and deepest desires that align with His. They can be love, justice, freedom, peace, rest, wholeness, honor, relationship, and respect.**

4. **These empower me to impact those around me.**

Here are the scriptural examples of FoF #17:

- John 12:1-8
- James 1:19-27
- Matthew 22:1-14
- 2 Timothy 2:8-19
- Philippians 4:8-9
- Psalm 37:4
- Galatians 5:22-23

Individual or Group Discussion Questions:

1. What concept or fact above made you think the most?

2. What person in the scriptural examples did you connect with the most?

3. What emotions were stirred within you? What is the source of that emotion?

FoF #18 – PLEDGE

I agree to be different and special.

As a part of the royal family of The Creator God and a citizen of His kingdom, your life must exhibit a noticeable difference. You are special to Him, and He desires the best for you. Jesus expects our loyalty and obedience. You must think and be different from what the culture expects or wants from you.

The Enemy will tell you that being a Believer and Follower of Jesus is the same as all other religious systems. It is not. It is unique and special, just like you.

Key points of FoF #18:

1. **I will live knowing that I am made In His Image.**

2. **I will choose to live my life as a temple of His Spirit.**

3. **I will not live as condemned but freed through the perfect gift of Jesus.**

4. **I will choose His will over the world's enjoyments.**

5. **My repentance will be continual.**

Here are the scriptural examples of FoF #18:

- 1 Peter 2:1-5
- 1 John 2:15-17
- John 8:3-11
- 2 Corinthians 6:14-7:1
- John 14:15
- Mark 8:36
- Matthew 25:1-13
- Hebrews 3:12-19
- James 1:19-27

Individual or Group Discussion Questions:

1. What concept or fact above made you think the most?

2. What person in the scriptural examples did you connect with the most?

3. What emotions were stirred within you? What is the source of that emotion?

FoF #19 – JOY

Jesus desires me to live in His ways with Joy and Peace.

The gift of His Spirit in our lives always leads us to a closer relationship with The Godhead and to the truth of Jesus. Your trust in Him will bring more joy and peace, but you may not feel it immediately.

He will lead you away from the wrong beliefs and behaviors that keep you in bondage. This separation can be difficult and may take longer than expected. However, once through this challenge, you will discover more peace and more joy in your life.

Key points of FoF #19:

1. **I rejoice in knowing that Jesus will always seek me, no matter how lost I am.**

2. **His pruning and correction are for our benefit.**

3. **His Spirit is the oil in the lamp of my life allowing me to shine with Joy.**

4. **My spirit and heart sing and shout in joy and peace.**

Here are the scriptural examples of FoF #19:

- John 15:1-11
- Luke 15:1-10
- Psalm 100
- Zephaniah 3:14-17
- John 17:6-26
- Isaiah 42:10-13
- Proverbs 20:27
- John 7:37-39
- Psalm 149
- John 4:9-14
- Isaiah 44:1-1-4
- Ezekial 47:7-12
- Psalm 126
- The Revelation 21:5-9
- The Revelation 22:1-7

Individual or Group Discussion Questions:

1. What concept or fact above made you think the most?

2. What person in the scriptural examples did you connect with the most?

3. What emotions were stirred within you? What is the source of that emotion?

FoF #20 – SERVED

Jesus served me, so I will serve you.

Jesus is the true example of a life lived in perfect understanding of The Creator God's will. His actions and words were always for the teaching and benefit of those around Him and for the future of His Kingdom. His love was so great for His many disciples. He humbled himself and served them, unlike any other scholars or masters.

He loves us just as much today. He serves us now through the work of His Spirit within us and through others. He will wash us, renewing and refreshing us in His Love, expressed as the living water. Experiencing this overflowing living water from Him will naturally lead us to share Him, His love, and serve others. His purpose in our serving others is not for recognition, but for both their benefit and ours.

Key points of FoF #20:

1. **Jesus is our example of service to one another in His love.**

2. **We are continually renewed through His washing with living water.**

3. **I desire for you to receive the same loving cleansing I received.**

Here are the scriptural examples of FoF #20:

- John 13:1-17
- John 12:24-26
- 1 Thessalonians 5:11:18
- John 4:7-24
- John 7:28-39
- Jeremiah 2:4-13

Individual or Group Discussion Questions:

1. What concept or fact above made you think the most?

2. What person in the scriptural examples did you connect with the most?

3. What emotions were stirred within you? What is the source of that emotion?

Group 3 – RESPONSE: *Deeper Questions*

The Deeper Questions below are meant for an in-depth study of this group. These questions can be completed any time after finishing Group 3 – RESPONSE.

1. Which of these basic understandings has a new meaning to you or resonated with you?

   ➢ A living relationship with Jesus awakens us.
   ➢ Our willing relationship is the response to His grace and love.
   ➢ Building our relationship with Jesus requires our active participation.
   ➢ Our relationship will change us. We will live differently than those in the world.

2. Which Foundation of Faith was most significant to you?

   FoF #14 – REBORN
   FoF #15 – PLANTED
   FoF #16 – UNDERSTANDING
   FoF #17 – IMPORTANCE
   FoF #18 – PLEDGED
   FoF #19 – JOY
   FoF #20 – SERVED

3. What in this study made it so significant?

4. In that significant Foundation of Faith, read at least one more Scriptural Example. Did this improve your understanding of it?

5. Why is **Salvation** part of His Spiritual Armor for us?

6. How does your understanding of The One True God differ after studying Group 3 – RESPONSE?

7. How will your relationships with other people change?

8. ***SPECIAL Homework - Preparation for FoF #21 - COMPASSION.**

   a) **With prayer, make a numbered list of every person or group who has hurt or wronged you through their words, actions, or beliefs.**

   b) **With prayer, make another numbered list of every person or group you have hurt or wronged through your words, actions, or beliefs.**

   c) **With prayer, make another numbered list of things you hate about yourself or need to change.**

FAITH - *Trust & Act*

Trusting His Sprit's leadings and acting on them is faith. As your faith is exercised, it empowers you to do more.

This is the fourth group of Foundations of Faith. Faith is acting as you believe. Acting is not just observing, but actively engaging with others and with Jesus. As your faith is used, you will be led to bigger and bolder acts.

He will equip and prepare us with everything we need to stand against The Enemy and take back what is promised to us. Our Faith in Him allows us to trust Him to do His part and releases us to focus on and do our part.

Here are the basic understandings for this group. They will be explored deeper in FoF #21 - #27:

The One True God gave all of us gifts He wants us to use.

As we use these gifts faithfully, he blesses us with more.

He wants our trust.

We trust The One True God to do His part, so we do not have to.

It is His part to exact judgement; it is our part to understand, forgive, and be available for others.

Wield the Shield of FAITH

Ephesians 6:16 "Above all, taking the shield of faith, wherewith ye shall be able to quench all the fiery darts of the wicked."

FoF #21 – COMPASSION

Our Forgiveness is Faith, and it is necessary.

Forgiving is the great breaker of bondage. We live each day in the present but with the results of every past decision and circumstance.

Our bodies have scars, muscle, and other features of our past eating, activities, and traumas. Our inner man has similar scars from our experiences. We have knowledge, beliefs, emotional or soul bonds, and can have spiritual bonds to our past. Some of these are beneficial to you and your relationships, and some are hindrances.

Forgiving breaks those negative bonds. Forgiving is like removing a splinter from your skin. If you do not remove it right away, it may remain there and be an inflamed and tender wound, or it may be encapsulated by your skin and become hard and a part of you. Without forgiving, you will be emotionally, spiritually, and maybe physically bound and ill.

Jesus wants to heal every part of you, the emotional, mental, spiritual, and potentially the physical wounds. Forgiving is critical for healing in your relationships, with Him, with yourself, and with others. Forgiving is a must.

Key points of FoF #21:

1. **Forgiving was originally a power only for The Godhead.**

2. **As His people, we are forgiven and now have the power and responsibility to forgive.**

3. When we forgive, we become released from the spiritual bondage and negative emotions in our soul.

4. We can forgive other people, groups, and even ourselves.

5. We can pray for other people to realize and experience their own forgiveness.

Here are the scriptural examples of FoF #21:

- Matthew 6:14-15
- Luke 11:1-4
- Psalms 51:3-13
- Matthew 18:21-35
- Acts 13:38-39
- Ephesians 4:31-32
- Colossians 3:12-15
- Psalm 86:1-5
- 1 John 5:14-17
- 2 Corinthians 2:9-11
- Job 1:4-5
- Luke 4:18-21
- Ezekiel 22:23-31
- Exodus 20

Individual or Group Discussion Questions:

1. What concept or fact above made you think the most?

2. What person in the scriptural examples did you connect with the most?

3. What emotions were stirred within you? What is the source of that emotion?

4. ***SPECIAL Homework -**

   a) **Forgive the numbered list of every person or group that has hurt or wronged you through their words, actions, or beliefs.**

   b) **Forgive yourself for the numbered list of every person or group that you have hurt or wronged through your words, actions, or beliefs.**

   c) **Forgive yourself for hating yourself and/or desiring a change in you, not from Jesus.**

   d) **Pray a blessing upon yourself and all those you listed previously. Allow His Spirit to heal every emotional, mental, spiritual and physical wounds.**

   e) **This can and should be repeated throughout your faith journey.**

   f) **Take time and honor your parents, no matter if forgiven or blessed in the above steps. Honor them whether they are living or dead and receive the special blessing.**

FoF #22 – TRUST

Our spiritual currency is obedience in faith and worship.

With any relationship, trust is crucial. You will not allow yourself to have a strong relationship with someone without it. All of us have been physically, mentally, or emotionally hurt by other people throughout our lives. This creates distrust in other individuals and other groups of people who look or act like those that have previously hurt us.

Our relationship with The Creator God and our trust in Jesus is reflected in our personal relationships and our activities during the day. Trusting Him gives us the freedom to obey Him and act in Faith even when we don't understand everything around us. He greatly desires these expressions of our relationship with Him.

Experiencing His love and protection invigorates us to worship Him. When we live in faith and worship, we will have a significant impact on Earth and in Heaven. We will desire to give or sacrifice our time and for His desires and the needs of others. This is what Paul refers to as a living sacrifice.

Key points of FoF #22:

1. **Faith is trusting and relying on The One True God for what may not be seen or understood.**

2. **Our Faith is what He needs to fulfill His purpose through us.**

3. **Faith means we act without doubt, without disbelief, and without knowing the result.**

4. **It was the servant's Faith that was rewarded by the master.**

5. **Our worship is offering ourselves in spirit and in Truth as a living sacrifice.**

Here are the scriptural examples of FoF #22:

- Hebrews 11:1-6
- James 2:1-4
- 1 Samuel 15:10-24
- 1 Chronicles 29:16-17
- Matthew 7:21-23
- The Revelation 14:12
- James 1:1-8
- Matthew 25:14-30
- Luke 19:11-27
- Psalms 51:15-17
- Matthew 8:5-22
- Romans 12:1-2
- John 4:21-24

Individual or Group Discussion Questions:

1. What concept or fact above made you think the most?

2. What person in the scriptural examples did you connect with the most?

3. What emotions were stirred within you? What is the source of that emotion?

FoF #23 – OUTREACH

Me serving you is my faith in action.

Serving one another is our natural response to His serving us. When you receive a gift, it is natural to share it. As Believers and Followers of Jesus, we are given the greatest gifts: His salvation, His life, His inheritance, His Spirit and much, much more.

These gifts are to be shared with those around you. His Spirit working within you is to be present, active, and shared. You cannot keep it like money to be used later. It is like you alone received an extremely large cake or 12 dozen cookies. You cannot enjoy all of it before you become ill or they become stale. When you share it, you receive the additional gift of experiencing the fellowship of others experiencing the same gifts.

Key points of FoF #23:

1. **We need Faith to act and to let His Grace flow through us.**

2. **Our response to receiving Him in our lives is to serve others as we were served.**

3. **As His representatives on Earth, we are to Serve others in His Name.**

4. **We are instructed to go out and create disciples, this is acting in Faith.**

Here are the scriptural examples of FoF #23:

- Romans 1:16-17
- Romans 10:14-18
- 2 Corinthians 5:16-21
- Ephesians 2:8-10
- Luke 10:25-37
- Matthew 25:31-46
- 2 Thessalonians 3:13-15
- Psalm 119:9-16
- Exodus 16:15-20

Individual or Group Discussion Questions:

1. What concept or fact above made you think the most?

2. What person in the scriptural examples did you connect with the most?

3. What emotions were stirred within you? What is the source of that emotion?

4. ***Special Homework –**

   a) **List the situations and people, including yourself, that you are currently complaining about or blaming.**

   b) **Repent of being hard or unsympathetic of them and/or yourself and ask His Spirit to bless every bit of you.**

FoF #24 – EMPOWER

When we take the keys, we can do anything with Jesus.

Keys unlock or lock doors, start or turn off engines, and open or close information. His power and authority are for us to use for our own lives and for others. Take them. Use them.

His unmeasurable love for us includes gifts for today, not just for the future in Heaven. He offers us the "keys" to the kingdom. This is His power and authority here on earth. We are to take these keys and use them.

Key points of FoF #24:

1. **Jesus, through His sacrifice and His Spirit, has given us the authority to work in His Name.**

2. **He has promised us His Spirit to lead and guide us.**

3. **We must take the authority given and use it in our lives.**

4. **The Grace and Power of The One True God flows through us.**

Here are the scriptural examples of FoF #24:

- Matthew 16:13-19
- 2 Kings 6:8-17
- John 16:5-15
- Matthew 19:16-26
- John 14:12-18
- Acts 4:32-33
- Mark 16:16-18
- Isaiah 11:1-2
- Zechariah 3:6-10
- The Revelation 5:1-7

Individual or Group Discussion Questions:

1. What concept or fact above made you think the most?

2. What person in the scriptural examples did you connect with the most?

3. What emotions were stirred within you? What is the source of that emotion?

FoF #25 – FREEDOM

Living in Faith and removing sin, sets us free.

Freedom, spiritual freedom, is living open to His Spirit's communication, unburdened by sin, influencing our lives. If we live within sin habitually, whatever it is, we will fight to keep that sin hidden or fight to keep it feeling normal. Just like cognitive dissonance, we will emotionally and may physically fight against it. We are likely unwilling to let go of the sin that we enjoy, even if we know we are trapped by it.

For some people, freedom feels like their greatest desire. For others, it is just a term to express rebellion. In part, they are both right. Since we live on a cursed earth, within many systems designed to keep us in bondage and out of The One True God's Word and will, our soul desires to be free of these and rebels against them.

Once you begin to experience spiritual freedom, you will want more and will seek it. This freedom will probably be contrary to how other people around you believe and the world's expectations. You will hear His Spirit more clearly. You will live more boldly in truth and ask for His guidance for your life.

Key points of FoF #25:

1. **All sin and unforgiveness are bondage.**

2. **The authority given to us is the key to removing this bondage.**

3. **Through our Faith and with His power, our confession and repentance of sin can remove it from our lives.**

4. **The more free we become, the less sin impedes us, the more we can help others be free.**

Here are the scriptural examples of FoF #25:

- Psalm 19:7-14
- Joshua 3:9-13
- Galatians 5
- Romans 8:1-4
- John 8:31-36
- Luke 15:1-10
- Philippians 2:12-15
- Isaiah 61:1
- Ephesians 4:17-32
- 2 Corinthians 6:14-7:1
- 1 John 1:5-10
- James 5:13-16
- 2 Corinthians 7:6-10

Individual or Group Discussion Questions:

1. What concept or fact above made you think the most?

2. What person in the scriptural examples did you connect with the most?

3. What emotions were stirred within you? What is the source of that emotion?

4. ***SPECIAL Homework - With earnest prayer, ask His Spirit to show you something restricting your spiritual freedom.**

FoF #26 – FIERCE

My fasting and fervent prayer moves heaven.

All our prayers are heard perfectly because of Jesus in Heaven. Then why fast and pray? Although you do not see them, The Enemy is continuously working against anyone with Jesus. However, our fasting and fervent prayers are powerful and can break through their opposition to us. Fasting and prayer are ways to use the keys to the kingdom that can affect the heavenly, unseen realms. These changes will alter things here on Earth.

Fervent prayer is the expression of a deep and meaningful desire. It is crying-out for help when you have no way to help yourself. It is your spirit desperate, as if you are chained and have no way to escape. Fervent prayer can be accomplished without fasting. However, fasting will always include fervent prayer.

Fasting is abstaining from solid food and potentially liquid nutrition. Fasting will cause physical discomfort and can make you weak. Any fast must be directed by His Spirit. You must know and consider your health limitations and medications when considering a fast. Seek His Spirit's guidance as to when, why, how long, and what you should fast to avoid any unnecessary health consequences. Consult your physician(s).

Key points of FoF #26:

1. **Our prayers are heard perfectly, no matter what words we use.**

2. **Fervent Prayer is not passive asking, it is praying with authority.**

3. **Fasting with prayer is a natural part of expressing our Faith.**

4. **His Spirit should lead when and how we are to fast with prayer.**

Here are the scriptural examples of FoF #26:

- James 5:13-18
- Matthew 17:14-21
- Matthew 6:16-18
- Romans 8:14-27
- Exodus 6:2-8
- Psalm 144:1-2
- 2 Chronicles 20:15-30
- Jude 1:17-21
- Hebrews 7:20-28

Individual or Group Discussion Questions:

1. What concept or fact above made you think the most?

2. What person in the scriptural examples did you connect with the most?

3. What emotions were stirred within you? What is the source of that emotion?

FoF #27 – HUNGER

We should hunger for all the spiritual gifts Jesus promised.

Hunger, great want, and covet are words to describe our soul's intense need for something. Paul specifically tells us we should intensely need and seek spiritual gifts. Spiritual gifts allow us to use His supernatural power for both ourselves and others.

These are necessary for our work with Jesus on Earth. He will give you these gifts sometimes consistently or sometimes during unique situations. No matter when or where, if you see a need for the gifts, ask for them and expect it, with no doubt. He desires to show His work through you.

Key points of FoF #27:

1. **All spiritual gifts are for the reborn Believers and Followers of Jesus.**

2. **Spiritual gifts are the manifestations of His anointing of power working through our faith.**

3. **The Godhead gives them to us to use as needed.**

4. **We need to desire spiritual gifts greatly and actively seek them.**

5. **As we obey Him and use them, we may receive more.**

Here are the scriptural examples of FoF #27:

- Acts 2:37-44
- Luke 11:9-13
- Acts 10:34-48
- Ephesians 1:15-23
- 1 Corinthians 14:1-4
- Acts 1:4-8
- 1 Corinthians 12:1-11, 27-31
- Acts 10:34-48
- James 4:7-10
- 1 Corinthians 14:13-19
- Romans 8:26-27
- Acts 8:14-17
- Matthew 3:1-12

Individual or Group Discussion Questions:

1. What concept or fact above made you think the most?

2. What person in the scriptural examples did you connect with the most?

3. What emotions were stirred within you? What is the source of that emotion?

4. ***SPECIAL Homework –**

a) Seek from the Scriptures and list all the spiritual gifts.

b) With earnest prayer, ask Him to give you a new spiritual gift.

c) If you receive this gift, praise and thank Him for it. Ask His guidance on when and where to use it.

d) He may confirm that something within you is not ready or is in your life preventing receiving gifts. If this occurs, praise and thank Him for the clarity.

e) This can and should be repeated throughout your faith journey.

Group 4 – FAITH: *Deeper Questions*

The Deeper Questions below are meant for an in-depth study of this group. These questions can be completed any time after finishing Group 4 – FAITH.

1. Which of these basic understandings has a new meaning to you or resonated with you?

   ➢ The One True God gave all of us gifts He wants us to use.
   ➢ As we use these gifts faithfully, he blesses us with more.
   ➢ He wants our trust.
   ➢ We trust The One True God to do His part, so we do not have to.
   ➢ It is His part to exact judgement; it is our part to understand, forgive, and be available for others.

2. Which Foundation of Faith was most significant to you?

   FoF #14 – REBORN
   FoF #21 – COMPASSION
   FoF #22 – TRUST
   FoF #23 – OUTREACH
   FoF #24 – EMPOWER
   FoF #25 – FREEDOM
   FoF #26 – FIERCE
   FoF #27 – HUNGER

3. What in this study made it so significant?

4. In that significant Foundation of Faith, read at least one more Scriptural Example. Did this improve your understanding of it?

5. Why is **Faith** part of His Spiritual Armor for us?

6. How does your understanding of The One True God differ after studying Group 4 – FAITH?

7. How will your relationships with other people change?

8. ***SPECIAL Homework –**

   a) **Have you already received any of His spiritual gifts?**

   b) **Which ones have you experienced through other people?**

JOURNEY - *Have a Living Relationship*

Go and journey where Jesus leads you.

This is the fifth group of Foundations of Faith. Having a very close relationship with anyone can be characterized as going for a walk or a journey with them. Our life with Jesus is the same. As we spend time with Him, we will grow in understanding and transform our character.

As He leads us, our responsibility, circumstances, and other relationships will change. What we will need from Him will change. On our journey, He will lead us to share the Good News in word and deed with others.

Here are the basic understandings for this group. They will be explored deeper in FoF #28 - #33:

Our journey is dangerous, full of temptations and obstacles.

Jesus illuminates our path.

Jesus is our guide and protector.

We are not alone on the Journey.

Our Journeys end in eternity.

Walk in the Shoes of The GOSPEL

Ephesians 6:15 "And your feet shod with the preparation of the gospel of peace;"

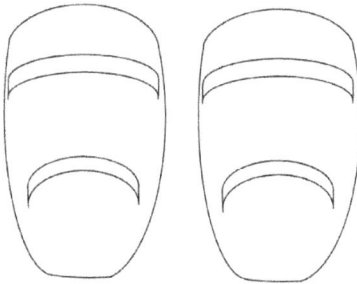

FoF #28 – WRESTLING

Our personal struggles are spiritual and specifically unique to our past and present.

All of us on earth have lives filled with struggles. If you do not struggle, then ask His Spirit, why not? We all wrestle with The Enemy and much more.

As we continue living our lives with The One True God, we will constantly and consistently be wrestling. This will be directly against enemy spirits and indirectly through other people under their influence. Additionally, we will struggle against our own harmful behaviors and beliefs.

His perfect will in our lives includes our separation from everything, not in His plan for us. As He leads your life, He wants you to rely on Him fully. He will likely lead you to wrestle with only one or two of these issues at a time. Preventing you from getting overwhelmed and giving up.

Key points of FoF #28:

1. **As we journey with Jesus, we will struggle because of our distorted world view and beliefs.**

2. **We will battle in ways unique to us and our past, yet similar to others.**

3. **These skirmishes are The Satan and his army working directly and indirectly against us.**

4. **Our difficulties can be overcome with His authority and wisdom in our lives.**

Here are the scriptural examples of FoF #28:

- Matthew 10:32-39
- James 4:1-10
- Romans 12:1-2
- 1 Corinthians 6:12-20
- 2 Timothy 2:1-4
- John 15:18-27
- 1 Timothy 4:1-10
- James 4:1-12
- Psalm 142
- John 5:12-14
- John 8:7-11

Individual or Group Discussion Questions:

1. What concept or fact above made you think the most?

2. What person in the scriptural examples did you connect with the most?

3. What emotions were stirred within you? What is the source of that emotion?

4. What are some current struggles in your life?

FoF #29 – CONNECTED

Abiding in Jesus is the heart of our daily relationship with Him.

Jesus referred to our relationship in a parable as abiding, like the branch to the grapevine. For those not familiar, this may seem odd and complex. Typically, wine grapes are cultivated with a vine and two large cordons, like a person standing with his arms up to the side in the shape of a cross.

We are those branches that bear the fruit. We must be connected to the vine, or we may become dead wood. If we are connected well, we will have much fruit that is a sweet food for others to be nourished and enjoyed. As we remain connected over time, our connection gets larger, our branch gets thicker, and can bear more fruit.

Key points of FoF #29:

1. **The Godhead desires relationships over empty works and practices.**

2. **Jesus and His Spirit are the vine that connects us to One True God.**

3. **Abiding is the act of continually receiving His living water.**

4. **We connect with Jesus through talking with Him, listening to Him, walking in the Spirit, and reading His Word.**

Here are the scriptural examples of FoF #29:

- Ephesians 5:1-14
- 1 Peter 5:8-11
- Proverbs 4:20-27
- 1 John 5:1-5
- Galatians 5:16-26
- John 7:37-39
- John 4:7-15
- John 15:1-8
- Matthew 12:36-37
- 1 Corinthians 10:20-21
- Hebrews 12:14-17
- 1 Corinthians 6:7-20
- Deuteronomy 30:15-20
- Ezekiel 37:24-28

Individual or Group Discussion Questions:

1. What concept or fact above made you think the most?

2. What person in the scriptural examples did you connect with the most?

3. What emotions were stirred within you? What is the source of that emotion?

FoF #30 – PROTECTED

We must wear His Spiritual Armor as we journey with Him.

Each study group references the pieces of His Spiritual Armor. Your spiritual armor is real in the spiritual realm. He has prepared for you multiple paths in your journey, depending on your willingness to go. You need the six armor pieces and prayer to follow Him and His path for you.

Your spiritual armor and praying in the spirit are both offensive and defensive. When it is in place, you will receive weapons against and protection from The Enemy. You can sense this spiritually, mentally, emotionally, and physically. You can also sense it in the same ways when it is not in place or damaged. Wear it daily. Let His Spirit guide you in utilizing them.

Key points of FoF #30:

1. **His Power goes forth and prepares the way for us.**

2. **We are given His Spiritual Armor to use in our journey.**

3. **His Spiritual Armor is an extension of The Creator God's power. It covers and is used by our spiritual body.**

4. **The parts of His Spiritual Armor are both defensive and offensive.**

5. **We should remember to put it on and to use it daily.**

Here are the scriptural examples of FoF #30:

- Ephesians 6:10-20
- 2 Corinthians 10:1-7
- John 8:12
- Exodus 15:1-13
- Deuteronomy 1:19-31
- Hebrews 5:1-11
- Numbers 10:35
- Luke 10:17-20
- Isaiah 37:33-36
- 1 Timothy 1:6-10

Individual or Group Discussion Questions:

1. What concept or fact above made you think the most?

2. What person in the scriptural examples did you connect with the most?

3. What emotions were stirred within you? What is the source of that emotion?

4. ***SPECIAL Homework –**

   a) **List the top 3-5 lies or negative thoughts that The Enemy sends to your mind.**

   b) **Repent of not rejecting these and allowing them to stay in your mind.**

   c) **Renounce these beliefs or thoughts and replace them with scriptural truths.**

   d) **This can and should be repeated throughout your faith journey.**

FoF #31 – COUNSEL

We should seek wisdom on our journey from both His Word and other believers.

In our faith journey, His Spirit will guide us to the answers in both His Word and with trusted counsel. Ask the questions; He is faithful to respond. He may lead you to find a particular passage or a series of passages in The Scripture.

He may lead you to seek another person for help. Specific people will aid you or give you counsel in understanding scripture. Or they may give you wisdom directly from His Spirit. These conversations can occur just once or frequently for many years.

These one-on-one discussions will have a spiritual purpose and possibly benefit both the soul and the body. Overall, it is wise to test what you have learned with multiple sources, spiritually or otherwise.

Key points of FoF #31:

1. **Seek wisdom in His Word.**

2. **We are to seek wise counsel from other believers we trust.**

3. **His Spirit will help us discern who will have words of wisdom or guidance.**

4. **As we grow in faith and understanding of His Word, we will also become wise counsel.**

Here are the scriptural examples of FoF #31:

- James 1:5-8
- Matthew 7:7-12
- Psalm 119:105-112
- Proverbs 1:1-7
- 1 Corinthians 2:7-16
- 1 John 4:1-3
- Deuteronomy 4:29-31
- The Revelation 1:1-3

Individual or Group Discussion Questions:

1. What concept or fact above made you think the most?

2. What person in the scriptural examples did you connect with the most?

3. What emotions were stirred within you? What is the source of that emotion?

FoF #32 – SUPPORT

He desires we live in community with like-minded believers.

All of us have a purpose within our communities. We should strive to be with others that believe as we do. This is not to discriminate or segregate, but to support one another better in the trials and tribulations of our lives.

He created humans to live together, not alone or in isolation. You should strive to find a community. With today's technology, internet, and digital connections, community does not need to be nearby, you can find others to join you from nearly anywhere.

Key points of FoF #32:

1. We were created to live in a support community.

2. This support community is The Body, His Community of the Called Out, (Church) on Earth.

3. We all have a purpose and tasks to fulfill within our support community.

Here are the scriptural examples of FoF #32:

- 2 Corinthians 6:14-18
- John 15:9-16
- James 5:7-12
- 1 John 1:5-7
- Acts 2:40-47
- Philippians 2:1-11

Individual or Group Discussion Questions:

1. What concept or fact above made you think the most?

2. What person in the scriptural examples did you connect with the most?

3. What emotions were stirred within you? What is the source of that emotion?

FoF #33 – HOME

We were created to live with Him as a community in Heaven on Earth.

From the beginning, humankind was created to live in community in a perfect relationship with The One True God. The Good News is that in the end, within the new heaven and earth, we will have the perfect existence as He intended.

As Believers and Followers of Jesus, we have His Spirit within us, and our spirit has that perfect relationship. But our soul and body don't and won't have perfection until the end. This incomplete existence creates a desire within our soul and sense in our bodies to be fully whole and with The Creator God. Many sense this as we get much older and examine our own mortality. We have the confidence that when our life ends, at its completion, we will join that perfect community with Jesus.

Key points of FoF #33:

1. **At creation humankind, was made to live in Heaven on Earth.**

2. **One day, we will have the perfect body living in Heaven on Earth.**

3. **In the end, we will be a community with Him, living out our purposes in harmony and communion.**

Here are the scriptural examples of FoF #33:

- 1 Thessalonians 4:13-18
- The Revelation 7:9-17
- The Revelation 21:1-7
- John 14:1-7
- 2 Corinthians 5:1-5
- Luke 23:39-43
- Isaiah 65:17-19
- 1 Corinthians 15:42-57
- Psalm 48

Individual or Group Discussion Questions:

1. What concept or fact above made you think the most?

2. What person in the scriptural examples did you connect with the most?

3. What emotions were stirred within you? What is the source of that emotion?

Group 5 – JOURNEY: *Deeper Questions*

The Deeper Questions below are meant for an in-depth study of this group. These questions can be completed any time after finishing Group 5 - JOURNEY.

1. Which of these basic understandings has a new meaning to you or resonated with you?

    ➤ Our Journey is dangerous, full of temptations and obstacles.
    ➤ Jesus is our guide and protector.
    ➤ Jesus illuminates our path.
    ➤ We are not alone on the Journey.
    ➤ Our Journeys end in eternity.

2. Which Foundation of Faith was most significant to you?

    FoF #28 – WRESTLING
    FoF #29 – CONNECTED
    FoF #30 – PROTECTED
    FoF #31 – COUNSEL
    FoF #32 – SUPPORT
    FoF #33 – HOME

3. What in this study made it so significant?

4. In that significant Foundation of Faith, read at least one more Scriptural Example. Did this improve your understanding of it?

5. Why is the **Gospel (Good News)** part of His Spiritual Armor for us?

6. How will your relationships with other people change?

7. Who is in your community of believers?

8. Why are you confident that you will be with Jesus in the end?

COMMITMENT - *Accept Jesus, then Share Him*

Keep your life focused on His Word and His Spirit and you will thrive with Jesus.

This is the sixth and last group of Foundations of Faith. It summarizes living with the understanding of our relationships with Jesus and others. Here is where our journey focuses outside of ourselves. We will see the results of our Faith in others. We will be tested again and again, each time gaining more and more ground for His kingdom.

The last Foundation of Faith is written as a vow. This is your commitment to trust Jesus with your present as well as your eternity and to live the life He has planned for you.

Here are the basic understandings for this group. They will be explored deeper in FoF #34 - #40:

Our relationship with Jesus requires a daily commitment to Him and each other.

We need to study The Bible/Scriptures and seek guidance to understand His plan for us.

We need other believers to help us with this commitment.

Use the Sword of the SPIRIT
and Pray in the SPIRIT

Ephesians 6:17-18 "...and the sword of the Spirit, which is the word of God: Praying always with all prayer and supplication in the Spirit..."

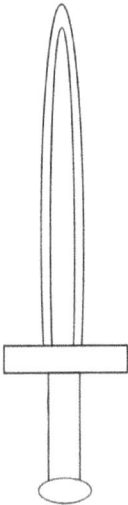

FoF #34 – BLESSED

We, the second born, the meek, and the humble, receive the blessing.

The One True God will almost always use those who the world would not expect or choose. He uses the humble, not the proud. He uses the meek, those with restrained strength, not the domineering. He uses the second born to gain the inheritance. He uses the "underdog" to win, like when a young David defeats and beheads a giant.

Our Creator God does not discard people. He will use our weaknesses to show His abilities and riches. He allows the hated and despised, tax collector and prostitute to lead, teach and be honored. He offers us that same grace and opportunity to be much more than The Enemy or others will allow.

Another analogy of our relationship with Him is that He is the potter, and we are the clay. He made us for a purpose. He will use us as we are now. He can give us a new purpose as often as needed. In this faith journey, He can always put us back on the potter's wheel and remake us, again and again.

Key points of FoF #34:

1. **He does not follow the ways of the world, and in His wisdom will choose who receives the blessing.**

2. **The humble and the meek are given honor and position.**

3. **In our weaknesses and imperfections, His strength and grace shows.**

4. **Like pottery, we are made for a purpose. And even if we have cracks, His Living water flows through them.**

5. **Unlike actual pottery, He can remake us as needed.**

Here are the scriptural examples of FoF #34:

- Genesis 27:1-29
- James 1:12-18
- 3 John 1:2-4
- 1 Samuel 17
- Genesis 48
- Matthew 5:1-12
- 1 Corinthians 1:18-31
- 1 Corinthians 3:18-23
- Jeremiah 18:1-6
- Romans 9:19-21

Individual or Group Discussion Questions:

1. What concept or fact above made you think the most?

2. What person in the scriptural examples did you connect with the most?

3. What emotions were stirred within you? What is the source of that emotion?

FoF #35 – CONTINUE

Stay the course through the trials and tribulations until we reign.

His Spirit led the writers of scripture to encourage us to keep persevering through everything. They confirm we should not quit. We should follow our personal journey, no matter what is happening to us or around us.

As we remain with Him, our lives will continually transform to be more like His. This commitment to follow and persevere through all the challenges of being separated from the world's way will be a journey full of life, joy, and peace.

Key points of FoF #35:

1. **Our continued time in relationship with Jesus will change us to be more like Him in thought, word, and deed.**

2. **This is a lifetime commitment, full of joy and peace, despite our struggles and separation from the world's ways.**

3. **We are to exercise our faith by continuing the journey.**

4. **Through perseverance, we will receive His Peace now and in the future.**

Here are the scriptural examples of FoF #35:

- Proverbs 29:18
- The Revelation 12:7-11
- Hebrews 12:1-2
- 1 Timothy 6:11-16
- 2 Peter 3:10-18
- 1 John 1:7-11
- Matthew 24:4-14
- Jude 1:2-3
- Galatians 6:1-10
- The Revelation 21:1-7

Individual or Group Discussion Questions:

1. What concept or fact above made you think the most?

2. What person in the scriptural examples did you connect with the most?

3. What emotions were stirred within you? What is the source of that emotion?

4. ***SPECIAL Homework –**

   a) **Ask Jesus to show you where your actions or beliefs are impeding your relationship with Him.**

   b) **Ask Him who or what in you may be resisting your relationship with Him.**

   c) **Commit to change.**

FoF #36 – ABUNDANCE

We are to share as He leads with joy and generosity.

As Jesus's Believers and Followers, we must give. Giving is an act of faith. We can give of our time, natural talents, spiritual gifts, property, or money. When we give of any or all of these, it shows Him that we fully trust in His promise to provide and care for us.

Give with joy from the abundance you have. However, we must let His Spirit guide us in all types of giving. Only He truly knows the plan for our physical, financial, and spiritual gifts. Only He knows the true needs of other individuals or groups.

Key points of FoF #36:

1. **Living in His Spirit brings responsibility.**

2. **We are to give cheerfully! The Creator God knows our hearts.**

3. **He has a plan for us. He will guide us as we give to others.**

Here are the scriptural examples of FoF #36:

- 1 Corinthians 13:1-13
- Luke 8:16-21
- Psalm 23:5-6
- Matthew 7:7-12
- Hebrews 4:14-16

Individual or Group Discussion Questions:

1. What concept or fact above made you think the most?

2. What person in the scriptural examples did you connect with the most?

3. What emotions were stirred within you? What is the source of that emotion?

4. ***SPECIAL Homework –**

   a) **Ask His Spirit to show you which of your gifts, physical or spiritual, to share.**

   b) **Then tomorrow, ask how much of it?**

   c) **Then the next day, ask for what length of time?**

   d) **Asking three separate times in three different ways allows His Spirit to confirm this within you. Commit to following His leading.**

FoF #37 – PURPOSE

At every moment, we have a unique purpose in the community of Jesus's Believers and Followers.

Jesus's Followers and Believers live in a special and unique relationship with Him and others. This is sometimes referred to as the "The Body of Christ." It is an ever-changing community of relationships serving and being served by one another.

In serving, we must trust His Spirit to guide us. Only He knows how long any one person will be in our lives. Some people will be beside us throughout our lives. Others could be there for just a few minutes.

At any moment, only He knows perfectly their needs or our needs. We must trust His guidance and the mission He has set before us. He may need us to lead or teach them or be led or taught by them. This dynamic is the beauty of living the community of "The Body of Christ."

Key points of FoF #37:

1. **In His Body, each person has a particular role to build up one another.**

2. **We are each gifted naturally and spiritually for our own growth and for others.**

3. **Our relationships with individuals and groups are specific to our personal mission.**

Here are the scriptural examples of FoF #37:

- 2 Timothy 4:1-5
- Romans 12:3-8
- 1 Corinthians 12:12-26
- Jeremiah 29:11-13
- 1 Timothy 4:12-16
- Ephesians 4:11-16
- Hebrews 6:1-7

Individual or Group Discussion Questions:

1. What concept or fact above made you think the most?

2. What person in the scriptural examples did you connect with the most?

3. What emotions were stirred within you? What is the source of that emotion?

FoF #38 – PARTNERS

Commitment to a small group of Jesus' Believers and Followers is necessary to maintaining strong relationships.

People crave intimate relationships. This is our soul expressing the desire for The One True God. With a few like-minded people as partners, we can do so much more. These relationships must have humility and the permission to be honest, so we can fulfill what we are led to do.

With these people, we give and receive encouragement, support, counsel, and more. You may be with them for decades, like a spouse. Or you can be with them for several years for general support in a group. Or you may be with them for just a few days on a specific mission. No matter how long or the purpose for the partners, they are an important part of your journey.

Key points of FoF #38:

1. **His Body is made of individuals and groups of individuals.**

2. **When we gather together, His Spirit is present.**

3. **When we share our lives humbly and honestly, our faith is strengthened.**

4. **We need to be committed to partners for support and encouragement.**

5. **We must give our partners permission to be honest with us.**

Here are the scriptural examples of FoF #38:

- 2 Thessalonians 2:1-15
- 1 Peter 4:8-11
- Galatians 6:1-3
- Mark 3:13-19
- Jude 1:20-23
- Ezekiel 32:30-31
- Proverbs 24:3-6

Individual or Group Discussion Questions:

1. What concept or fact above made you think the most?

2. What person in the scriptural examples did you connect with the most?

3. What emotions were stirred within you? What is the source of that emotion?

FoF #39 – COMFORT

We receive comfort and rest. We should give comfort and rest.

The Creator God rested on the seventh day. He also commanded the Hebrews to rest on the sabbath days. The land rested during each seventh year and the 50th Jubilee year.

The challenges of being a Jesus Believer and Follower are continuous and sometimes overwhelming. This is why His Spirit is our comfort and rest. We need to recover from the work or battles we experience.

As we receive comfort and rest, we should give comfort and rest to one another. This can be as giving comfort or sharing the burden for one another. Or it can be spiritual by "standing in the gap" on the front line of their battle or "going to the throne" for them, giving them rest.

Key points of FoF #39:

1. **Jesus is Lord, and through Him, we receive comfort and rest.**

2. **His Spirit is our Comforter for all our days.**

3. **Rest is more than physical. It is mental, emotional, and spiritual.**

4. **We are to give comfort and rest to one another.**

5. **The Jubilee Year was the year of rest for the land and all debts were forgiven.**

Here are the scriptural examples of FoF #39:

- Romans 8:26-30
- Hebrews 4
- Psalm 37:1-11
- Matthew 11:25-30
- Ezekial 22:23-30
- Hebrews 3:1-6
- 2 Thessalonians 1:3-10
- Matthew 12:1-8
- Isaiah 40:31
- Isaiah 28:4-12

Individual or Group Discussion Questions:

1. What concept or fact above made you think the most?

2. What person in the scriptural examples did you connect with the most?

3. What emotions were stirred within you? What is the source of that emotion?

FoF #40 – COMMIT

We will commit to journey side by side with Jesus.

Our relationship with Jesus, The Godhead, has had several analogies revealed throughout the 40 Foundations of Faith©. Each one has its own challenges and benefits, and each fully exists at the same time.

- Father to a Child
- King to a Prince/Princess
- Husband to a Bride
- Gardener to a Plant
- Vine to a Branch
- Potter to the Clay

To live in these relationships, you must accept Jesus as your Savior, and allow His Spirit to reside within your body. Your acceptance allows you to experience a spiritual rebirth. Paul explains this as your spirit is married to His Spirit. With our rebirth, we inherit all He has, supernatural gifts, protection, provision, and guidance.

If you want this beautifully intricate and diverse relationship with Him, take this moment and proclaim your commitment.

Key points of FoF #40:

1. **Living as a believer and follower of Jesus is a covenant, a commitment, and a relationship.**

2. **He is the Way; if you are willing proclaim, "I will Walk in His Way."**

3. **He is the Truth; if you are willing proclaim, "I will Abide in His Truth."**

4. **He is the Life; if you are willing proclaim, "I will Live through His Life."**

Here are the scriptural examples of FoF #40:

- John 14:1-7
- Matthew 28:16-20
- Mark 16:15-20
- Luke 24:44-53
- 1 Peter 2:1-10
- Leviticus 25:8-17
- Hebrews 10:19-25
- 1 John 2:1-6
- 1 Samuel 12:20-25
- John 4:10-26
- Ephesians 1:13-21
- The Revelation 19:6-8
- 2 Timothy 2:19

Individual or Group Discussion Questions:

1. What person in the scriptural examples did you connect with the most?

2. What emotions were stirred within you? What is the source of that emotion?

Group 6 – COMMITMENT: *Deeper Questions*

The Deeper Questions below are meant for an in-depth study of this group. These questions can be completed any time after finishing Group 6 - COMMITMENT.

1. Which of these basic understandings has a new meaning to you or resonated with you?

   ➢ Our relationship with Jesus requires a daily commitment to Him and each other.
   ➢ We need to study the Bible/Scriptures and seek guidance to understand His plan for us.
   ➢ We need other believers to help us with this commitment.

2. Which Foundation of Faith was most significant to you?

   FoF #34 – BLESSED
   FoF #35 – CONTINUE
   FoF #36 – ABUNDANCE
   FoF #37 – PURPOSE
   FoF #38 – PARTNERS
   FoF #39 – COMFORT
   FoF #40 – COMMIT

3. What in this study made it so significant?

4. In that significant Foundation of Faith, read at least one more Scriptural Example. Did this improve your understanding of it?

5. Why are the **Spirit and Word** part of His Spiritual Armor for us?

6. How will this change how your relationship with Jesus?

7. How will your relationships with other people change?

8. ***SPECIAL Homework Recap - Are there areas of Special Homework His Spirit wants you to go deeper?**

    a) **How will you take the time needed to maintain a relationship with Him (FoF #6)?**

    b) **Should you to be baptized (FoF #14)?**

    c) **Should you forgive more and pray for others (FoF #22)?**

    d) **Do you complain or blame anyone or anything (FoF #23)?**

    e) **Are there people or things that restrict your spiritual freedom (FoF #25)?**

    f) **Are there spiritual gifts you deeply desire (FoF #27)?**

    g) **Are there more religious issues in your life (FoF #30)?**

    h) **Are there more beliefs you hold that impede your relationship with Him (FoF #35)?**

    i) **Are there more gifts you should share (FoF #36)?**

Congratulations! You have completed the study.

If you still have doubts about "all this Jesus stuff," then ask His Spirit to show you why. Listen for an answer. Ask His Spirit to come into you. Be His and be free.

If you have recommitted or committed your life to The One True God, then celebrate! If you have deepened your understanding of the foundations of His Truth, then praise Him. If you struggled with some of the Deeper questions, go back to them and seek Him.

Just like the 3-Day weekends, Jubilee Days was designed to be experienced more than once. This study is also designed to be repeated. I urge you to schedule time in the coming days to review either the same study again or the alternative study on the next pages.

The Way, Truth & Life – *An Alternate Study Option*

When developing Jubilee Days and the 40 Foundations of Faith©, I kept asking Him how He wanted the event to finish. He confirmed He wanted us to commit, as in John 14:6:

"Jesus saith unto him, I am the way, the truth, and the life: no man cometh unto the Father, but by me."

As you recall, this is primarily how FoF #40 reads.

Once the end was clear, The Way, Truth, and Life, His Spirit guided me to summarize our lives as Jesus's Believers and Followers into precepts. A precept a principle or general rule to live by. This scripture states we should also learn by precept. Isaiah 28:9-10 states:

"Whom shall he teach knowledge? and whom shall he make to understand doctrine? them that are weaned from the milk, and drawn from the breasts. For precept must be upon precept, precept upon precept; line upon line, line upon line; here a little, and there a little: For with stammering lips and another tongue will he speak to this people."

The following is a list of precepts for you. The precepts are more encompassing and correlate to several FoF groups. Each one has several corresponding of the 40 Foundations of Faith©. The order they follow differs from the study. It is another way to study the same FoF in a broader topical manner.

In His Way
Be Partners with Him and fellow Believers

We strive to live in the spirit, continually seeking His Spirit for His will and His Spiritual Gifts in our lives.

Refer to: Group 1 FoF #01 & #06, Group 2 FoF #12, Group 3 FoF #15, Group 4 FoF #24 & #27, Group 5 FoF #29 & #30, and Group 6 FoF #34.

Living with His Spirit adds true joy and purpose to our lives and a love for all people.

Refer to: Group 1 FoF #02 & #05, Group 2 FoF #11, Group 3 FoF #14 & #19, Group 4 FoF #21 & #23, Group 5 FoF #32, and Group 6 FoF #38.

He has a purpose for us. He will lead us where to go, but we must take the first step for His power to show. It is our faith that allows The Creator God's grace to become visible. Faith is like a muscle that grows in strength as it is continually used and stretched.

Refer to: Group 1 FoF #06, Group 2 FoF #10, Group 3 FoF #18 & #20, Group 4 FoF #22, #23 & #25, Group 5 FoF #29, and Group 6 FoF #36.

When everything is made new again, Jesus's believers and followers will inherit the earth and live in perfect harmony with one another and His new creation.

Refer to: Group 1 FoF #03, Group 2 FoF #13, Group 3 FoF #20, Group 4 FoF #25, Group 5 FoF #32 & #33, and Group 6 FoF #34, #36 & #39.

In His Truth
Seek Truth in The Scripture

Scriptures are the words of The One True God, written by humans, to their audience and for us today.

Refer to: Group 1 FoF #01, #04 & #05, Group 2 FoF #09, Group 3 FoF #16, Group 5 FoF #29 & #31, and Group 6 FoF #39 & #40.

In the Garden of Eden, humans disobeyed and allowed sin to separate us from perfect communion with The Creator God and eternal life. We gave our authority to Lucifer.

Refer to: Group 1 FoF #02, #03 & #04, Group 2 FoF #07, #08 & #13, Group 3 FoF #14, Group 4 FoF #24, Group 5 FoF #33.

The Satan's authority and power remains in the world today. Jesus' sacrifice fulfilled the law and paid for our sin, allowing our return to His authority.

Refer to: Group 1 FoF #03 & #04, Group 2 FoF #07, #08, #09, & #10, Group 3 FoF #14, Group 4 FoF #25, Group 5 FoF #28.

We face more struggles because of our separation from The Enemy's system and beliefs. The Creator God gave us His Spiritual Armor and His gifts to overcome and persevere through our struggles.

Refer to: Group 2 FoF #7 & #8, Group 3 FoF #15, Group 4 FoF #24 & #27, Group 5 FoF #28, #30 & #32, and Group 6 FoF #35.

We use His Spiritual Armor for both defense and offense with The Enemy.

Refer to: Group 2 FoF #13, Group 3 FoF #18, Group 4 FoF #24 & #26, Group 5 FoF #28 & #30, and Group 6 FoF #35, #37 & #40.

In His Life
Be in Covenant relationship with The Godhead

The scriptures clearly show The Creator God made both heavenly/spiritual beings and earthly beings.

Refer to: Group 1 FoF #01, #02 & #04, Group 2 FoF #07 & #13, Group 4 FoF #26 & #27, Group 5 FoF #28 & #33.

He created us in His image, to be His ruling family on Earth. We are to accept this importance and share His gifts as directed.

Refer to: Group 1 FoF #02, Group 2 FoF #11 & #13, Group 3 FoF #20, Group 4 FoF #23, Group 5 FoF #33, and Group 6 FoF #34, #36 & #39.

The Godhead desires a relationship with us. Throughout The Scripture, this relationship is exemplified as a husband and wife and father and child. We should desire to live with Him continuously.

Refer to: Group 1 FoF #03 & #05, Group 2 FoF #11 & #12, Group 3 FoF #16, #17 & #18, Group 5 FoF #33, and Group 6 FoF #40.

To return to the great relationship, we must accept His gift of grace through faith. Then we must abide in Him and follow His Word and plan for us.

Refer to: Group 1 FoF #05 & #06, Group 2 FoF #10 & #12, Group 3 FoF #15 & #17, Group 4 FoF #21 & #25, Group 5 FoF #29.

We communicate with Him and His Spirit through our heart, which is our inner self, mind, conscience, and spirit.

Refer to: Group 1 FoF #05 & #06, Group 3 FoF #16, Group 4 FoF #22 & #26, Group 5 FoF #29 & #31, and Group 6 FoF #38 & #40.

Our misguided beliefs and sin interfere with our communication and relationship with Him. As we change to better conform to His will, we will hear His Spirit more clearly and will experience more of Him in our lives.

Refer to: Group 1 FoF #05 & #06, Group 2 FoF #11, Group 3 FoF #14 & #19, Group 4 FoF #21 & #25, Group 5 FoF #28, and Group 6 FoF #37.

Living in the spirit

Living a life connected to His Spirit is beautiful and full of purpose. I trust His plan for my life, and it is a joy to follow His leadings as directed. There is always a blessing on the other side of trusting and acting, sometimes immediately but often delayed. Sometimes, His Spirit will tell you to wait before continuing. Here is one of those times, where I just needed to wait.

Early in my studies, I had asked Him to "baptize" me with "fire." For many religious systems, this is an odd statement. In its simplest terms is to be given spiritual gifts. During that time of studying, I read where Paul directs in several letters to "live in spirit." And Jesus stays in John 4:24:

"God is a Spirit: and they that worship him must worship him in spirit and in truth."

This verse has been the cornerstone verse of my life ever since.

As Jesus's Believers and Followers, we have the greatest gift of YHWH, His Spirit, living within us. I envision it as our spirit in continual communion with His Spirit, as one spirit, similar to our marriages being described as one flesh.

We are created to live moment by moment with Him. However, we live in our bodies on this earth. All of us with distractions and temptations. These pressures can lead to behaviors of sin and impede us from living with His Spirit. They burden us and restrict our freedom. They become, as Charles Dickens calls, "we forge the chains we wear in life."

Early in 2023 while reading The Revelation, I was struck by a peculiar part of John's vision where there are a series of sevens. 5:6 states this:

"And I beheld, and, lo, in the midst of the throne and of the four beasts, and in the midst of the elders, stood a Lamb as it had been slain, having seven horns and seven eyes, which are the seven Spirits of God sent forth into all the earth."

In our current US Christian culture, we are taught that there is the one Holy Spirit, not seven. I immediately completed a word search within scripture for "seven." I do this frequently to see the many examples of the same phrases or words are there, similar the "Why 40?" chapter. I could not find "seven Spirits of God." So, I asked for more understanding. His Spirit confirmed not yet, but soon.

A few months later, on May 16, 2023, while studying "the branch" of Jesse, He led me to Isaiah 11. This is where the prophet lists the Seven Spirits, without using the word seven. So, it was not so easily found.

When I read the list of Spirits in Isaiah, I found it confusing. The King James version uses terms that seemed too similar in our English to make sense. So, I went to the Hebrew descriptions and prayed and asked for clarity. He gave it to me.

Here is the King James translation, the Hebrew and His clarification to me:

King James	Hebrew	His Clarification
Spirit of the Lord	ruah YHWH	His Spirit
Wisdom	hakma	Skillfulness
Understanding	bina	Discernment
Counsel	esa	Advice
Might	gebura	Valor
Knowledge	da'at	Awareness
Fear of the Lord	yir'a	Reverence & Respect

When reviewing this list, I determined that a person "Living in spirit" lives life in this way:

- They live with continual **Reverence & Respect** of The One True God and **His Spirit** within.
- They have a mind actively **Aware** of the natural and supernatural world.
- They see and seek spiritual **Discernment** and **Advice**.
- As needed, they use supernatural **Skillfulness** and **Valor**.

When you compare this clarification of the seven "Spirits of God" to Jesus, you can understand why Paul wrote in Colossians 2:9-10:

"For in him dwelleth all the fulness of the Godhead bodily. And ye are complete in him, which is the head of all principality and power:..."

While here on earth, Jesus demonstrated a life lived with all the Spirits of God. This is how we should live each and every moment.

What is the Jubilee Days?

Much of this book is entirely due to the mission He set upon me to lead a team through the developing Jubilee Days. This has taken several years, and soon we will start these events. He wanted me to write this book before finishing the various workbooks for Jubilee Days, which admittedly, made no sense to me. However, he does not ask us to understand, but to listen and obey. Doing so is faith.

Jubilee Days was developed by a team of experienced leaders from several different 3-Day movements. The 3-Day movements I am familiar with are products of the Catholic Cursillo. These events, commonly called "weekends," typically start on Thursday evening and continue to Sunday evening. They involve three days of worship, sharing, and teaching by laypersons and ministers. There are 33 key points examined, shared, and explained through personal testimony. Throughout, participants are served by other men and women sharing the Gospel and grace.

These weekends attempt to be an example of sharing the Truth in Love, like Paul told the Ephesians in 4:15-16:

> *"But speaking the truth in love, may grow up into him in all things, which is the head, even Christ: From whom the whole body fitly joined together and compacted by that which every joint supplieth, according to the effectual working in the measure of every part, maketh increase of the body unto the edifying of itself in love."*

And Jude writes 1:20-23:

"But ye, beloved, building up yourselves on your most holy faith, praying in the Holy Ghost, keep yourselves in the love of God, looking for the mercy of our Lord Jesus Christ unto eternal life. And of some have compassion, making a difference: And others save with fear, pulling them out of the fire; hating even the garment spotted by the flesh."

"Weekends" are held throughout the world in many countries and languages. There have been millions of individuals who have attended and served at these events. It is both a service ministry and a discipleship opportunity for faith growth. There are dozens of different roles and functions to take part in and grow from. In Via de Christo, one of the Lutheran versions of the Cursillo, I found it to be both a ministry and a place to grow in faith.

A Jubilee Days event is like a Cursillo based 3-Day weekends. But, in many ways, it is not. Primarily, Jubilee Days events were expected to serve those brothers and sisters in retirement and care facilities. Because of these challenging living conditions, the event occurs in six short days spread over two weeks, not three long days.

Each 4-hour day has only four different Talks or parts. Any believer living or working at these facilities can attend and invite guests. The goal is to build a support community within the facility. Additionally, Jubilee Days has been designed to be held virtually and can be set up for other facilities or groups.

The Cursillo-based 3-Day Weekends were expected to serve persons already in an active church community with a pastor/minister to return to for guidance and leadership. Since people living in a retirement or other facility will likely have no church community, Jubilee Days expanded the 3-Day's 33 key points into the more comprehensive 40 Foundations of Faith©. This would fill in the missing information and understandings of a typical church community.

These lessons are shared within Talks from either laypersons or ministers. In a Jubilee Days event, the 40 Foundations of Faith© as shown in this book, would be shared with Guests prior to the event. This is intended not to replace the sharing, but to prepare them to focus more on the testimony and less on the facts.

Due to the limitations of time, layperson Foundations of Faith are shared in pairs. And those shared by ministers include a brief worship service. Most of the FoF would be covered in about six minutes, each with one scriptural example. The person shares The FoF as an example within their life, not taught. After each person shares their testimony, then a small group discussion would follow.

Jubilee Days events are designed to be held onsite at the facilities or online. This differs from the standard 3-Day movement, where participants and the serving team are sequestered. To assist with continuity of the event and lessons learned, each day of a Jubilee Days event ends with homework. Several of these questions are very personal and are to help an individual into a deeper relationship with The One True God.

As noted earlier, most of this book was designed for Jubilee Days. However, His Spirit clarified He intended this work to be much more. Like the 3-Day weekends, knowledge shared without the testimony of someone sharing it, has little meaning. This is why 3-Days weekends have so much impact. If you are interested, please visit thejubileedays.com.

My Journey

I have found that a journey with Jesus is like a person living out their days in a novel with a confirmed "happily ever after." There are days of great exploration, battles, great romance, and days of supreme rest. This can be true for everyone. All of us can live in the ebb and flow of His great love story.

As a Jesus Believer and Follower, life on earth is the most challenging and yet the most rewarding. In microeconomics, the greater the risk, the greater the reward. But with Him, the risk may feel great, but it is only temporary, and the reward is immeasurable. To receive the reward, you must choose to accept Him and His will for you. Then you will appreciate your role in the real eternal challenge.

I see my life as simple and yet complex. I was born in the late sixties and grew up in rural Indiana, near my extended family. I fell in love with Susan at college, then married her just afterward. Later in life, I rediscovered Jesus. He was still just the same as I remembered from my youth.

Just like everyone else, I struggled with all the temptations of this life and succumbed to many. I have spent most of my life making decisions based on money and its deceitful freedom. This and other sins have caused broken relationships with friends and family, and I have several times barely kept my marriage.

You may argue that as we age, we see life differently. This is true. We see it through a perspective of decades, not years. We are also inclined to forget the grind of life, and only the highlights remain. I have shared some of these highlights here. As time passes, year after year, the struggles we experienced seem further away. And now that I am one of His, I see His presence and peace becoming closer.

Originally, I felt the need to be anonymous with this book and its intimate contents of my testimony. One Saturday, Susan and I discussed the potential for a pen name. She told me "Be bold. He will keep us protected from whatever there is." Now, as with most times, I have "tested the spirits" and have my "two or three witnesses."

The morning before, His Spirit reminded me of a previous personal mission statement where I wrote, something similar to "be as Bold as Peter, as Wise as Paul, and with a worshipful heart as David." And just the day before that, I found:

Psalm 27:5:

"For in the time of trouble he shall hide me in his pavilion: in the secret of his tabernacle shall he hide me; he shall set me up upon a rock."

And as I write this, I was reminded of the vision of A.A. Allen where he sees us, the remnant of His church, protected in the cliff face like in Job 39:27-28 and The Revelation 12:14.

So, I will be as my beloved encouraged me and continue to strive to be like those men. She and I are confident Jesus will do with us and this study as He desires, no matter what The Enemy brings.

My Early Years

I was raised in the heart of rural farm country, with both parents, my maternal grandparents, aunts, uncles, and cousins. Everyone was within a reasonable bike ride. With farming communities, the land is as much a part of the family as the people. In 1974, our family built our house less than a 5-minute walk from our grandparents. We never moved.

My younger sister, Abbi, and I spent almost every weekend with our grandparents for much of my elementary & junior high school years. Our two houses were the constant. And although grandma and grandpa have passed, my sister now lives in their house. And our much younger brother Erik, now lives with our parents, the same 5-minute walk away.

In 1979, during my third-grade year, my classmates and I lined up preparing to leave for the Easter weekend. My teacher, a strong Christian woman, told me "I envy you. You will see Jesus when He returns." Although that was nearly 50 years ago, that moment is still very clear to me today. She and her husband were my teachers for four full years until I left for the Jr./Sr. high school.

Her statement has been with me my whole life. Was it a moment of prophecy over me? Or was it just the heart of a good woman expressing her concern for the changing culture? Either way, in the deepest recesses of my mind and soul, I still believe it.

Should this great revelation have spurred me to throw all caution away? Yes! Should a true Believer and Follower of Jesus and of scripture just say no to everything the world has and evangelize on the street corner? Yes! However, I did not. My soul sometimes wants to do it. But right now, I am writing these words and trusting His will to be done on "earth as it is in heaven."

Lured Away and Finding Him Again

I was raised in a Swedish Lutheran Church, surrounded by fields of soybeans and corn. It was comfortable and safe. Similar to other farming communities, most families at the church were distant relatives.

My entire childhood experience with church was there. We occasionally made it to other churches, but only for special occasions or a cooperative youth week. After I completed my Confirmation, I noticed the changes within.

Most cultures have "a rite of or passage" for young men and women. This represents their "age of accountability." Many of us experience it in our early teens. Our experiences and our relationship with adults change.

As a child, we believe the many fairytales, Santa, and other myths. Then we discover other lies told by adults like "we are all equal" and "you are special." As these lies become more and more clear, we start to mistrust any and all adults.

Once I hit that age of accountability, I mostly just kept going on the path my parents and grandparents taught me: do good, be good, and learn in school. But I had real questions with no answers. Then, I found new freedom with my job and a car.

I discovered I could turn the pent-up inward protection predominant in my life into outward rebellion, but I kept it secret. My rebellion was a bittersweet cocktail. I explored without supervision, stayed out late until the dawn, hung around with older teens and adults, and experienced drugs and alcohol.

My years of rebellion were not just against adults, schools, then later with my bosses, but against The One True God. Unfortunately, I had become of the age where my actions had consequences. I was old enough to know better and was accountable. At that age, we all have to live with the consequences of our decisions in our spirits, souls, and bodies.

I was no longer under the spiritual protection of my father, my family's spiritual head. Without this protection, I felt freer to explore more, not only emotionally, but spiritually, and left behind my church teachings. I discovered and started experimenting with occult, wiccan, and eastern meditation practices.

Then I graduated from high school and left for college. It was a disaster. I discovered more drugs, alcohol, and young witches altogether to tempt and distract me. Additionally, I discovered that I was now no longer the smart kid in a small town. I was the uneducated, unconnected, poor kid full of prejudice, experiencing college with the "privileged" upper middle class.

I was not who I thought I was. The rebellious spirit within me made my life on campus very difficult. I had desired to be an artist or writer, but discovered that was a world in which I did not fit. My rebellion quickly became depression. Instead of lashing out, all I did was smoke and watch MTV.

Under the influence of witches and the occult, I had several intense dreams of being the wielder of good magick fighting those with dark magick. I had no concept back then of how spiritually dangerous those practices were. Since then, I have fully repented of these sins, asked Jesus to forgive me, and broken all the curses associated with them.

I did not return to school the next fall. Instead of driving to college, I drove off to pursue a "vision quest." I desired to experience the same exciting life in the supernatural as Carlos Casteneda wrote about in Mexico. I wanted the thrill of being a part of something more than just an ordinary life.

I decided my vision quest would include visits to all the sacred sites of the Southwest. However, I stopped in Greers Ferry Lake, Arkansas and found a part-time job in landscaping. They paired me with a part-time pastor.

Of course, being the young man from Indiana, in Arkansas, he asked what I was doing there. I said plainly, "I was seeking." Thinking back, to an evangelist, those sing like golden words to an open door. He directed me to the Truth of Jesus I had so eagerly dismissed as another lie taught to me by my parents or society.

He gave me a small copy of the New Testament, which I read in my tent and car. Yes, I lived cheaply in a tent and a small '83 Pontiac Sunbird. He instructed me to read the Gospel of John. To date, this is still one of my best decisions. While reading, my spirit kept pointing to the reality of Jesus. I found within me that heart which loved Jesus as a child before I was led away from my faith.

A couple of weeks later, I proclaimed my acceptance of Him at a Billy Graham crusade in Little Rock. The next week, the lovely people at the small local Church of Christ fully immersed me in a baptism that I desperately desired.

After leaving Arkansas, I continued my vision quest, but with a new purpose. I would no longer seek the truth like Carlos Castenda in spirit animals brought to me through peyote. I needed to know what I would do now, with Jesus.

I spent weeks stopping at places in the deserts of New Mexico and Arizona. The desert was indescribable. Beauty draped with starkness. The multi-colored soils and cliffs were dotted with many shades of green. The stars at night were brilliant and vast, far greater than my imagination. And horizontal lightning was unlike any I had ever seen. The desert was grand, rocky, sparse, and yet, full of life.

While driving south through the Painted Desert in Arizona, the local classical music station played the William Tell Overture. With this musical score in my car and the windows open, I prayed while looking at the beauty of the desert. His Spirit began to show me what was next. He confirmed I should follow my desires to be a builder.

The decision that day to trust His Spirit started me on the path to a life of continuous change. The challenges and great joys began. I continued to visit several of the remaining sacred sites. In Sedona, I witnessed other seekers clinging to the rocks, absorbing spiritual vortex energy. I tried it, but it had no meaning. I already had His Spirit within. It just affirmed for me that finding Jesus again was my vision quest fulfilled.

The Valleys and Mountain Tops

That next fall, I started over at Purdue University with purpose, two good friends, and Jesus. I thought I had it all together, ready to restart my life. In the collegiate environment, I quickly lost the faith in Jesus I had gained just months before. I acted just like the thousands of students around me, becoming ambivalent about my faith. With disillusionment in my heart, I proclaimed there was no God.

I was the rocky soil Jesus describes and discusses through the parable of the Sower.

Luke 8:5-8

*"A sower went out to sow his seed: and as he sowed, some
fell by the way side; and it was trodden down, and the
fowls of the air devoured it. And some fell upon a rock;
and as soon as it was sprung up, it withered away,
because it lacked moisture. And some fell among thorns;
and the thorns sprang up with it, and choked it. And other
fell on good ground, and sprang up, and bare fruit an
hundredfold. And when he had said these things, he cried,
He that hath ears to hear, let him hear."*

My spiritual strength and belief quickly withered away.
Not only did I confirm there was no God, but all spirituality
was just a fairytale. I told myself that the entire year before; I
was a fool.

So, I declared myself no longer Christian, but an atheist
living a purely logical life. This time my life would be simpler. I
would not be manipulated by religion and would be free to
do as I selfishly wanted. Like those other wiccan and eastern
practices, this was spiritually damaging. Thankfully, although I
was declaring myself an atheist, I truly was not. Jesus never
let me go so far away from Him, that I did not see myself
coming back.

Then in the next year on August 23, 1991, I met Susan. She was the woman I had always wanted. During my vision quest, I read books on various topics, several on relationships and made a list of six characteristics I wanted within my wife. Quickly, I realized she had all six and declared my love was just not attraction for the moment, but I would love her for a lifetime. We decided on a wedding date approximately two weeks later.

We were married just after my graduation in my home church in the country. After our wedding in 1993, we immediately moved out of the state. Early on, our marriage was full of joy, but it had many relational challenges between us and our families. Most of these would have led other couples to divorce. Except, from the beginning, we committed to one another that quitting was not an option.

Eventually, I took my relationship with Jesus and Susan seriously and steadily cleaned out my selfish beliefs and behaviors. Today, I have no doubt, Jesus allowed us to find one another and today still blesses our life together. Although The Enemy has made us question it repeatedly, His Spirit has shown us the truth within each other that we were meant for one another.

It is an injustice to summarize our marriage in just these few scattered paragraphs. The truth of what a strong relationship needs to thrive from both partners, is far beyond these highlights. It is a lifetime of commitment and recommitments to each other.

In college, my direction to be a builder turned into the desire to be a contractor. I had eventually become a minor partner within a startup commercial door company, which ended badly. They fired me, just before Christmas of 1999. Through that never leaving spirit of rebellion, I made a series of bad choices leading me there. After a few months of freelance work, I decided I no longer wanted to be a contractor. I wanted to learn the other side of the building equation.

While trying to discern how to get there, I remembered I worked on a school renovation project that had the best architectural drawings I had ever seen, right here in Indianapolis. So, I went to that architect and found an opportunity in their construction management team ready for me. It was a group of Christians, designing, and building churches and church campuses. Jesus was guiding my way, before I had even started seeking Him.

During that time with them, there was no doubt my habits took me the furthest away from a good man I had ever been. But working with them and all the various congregations stirred up a missing part of me. The group I worked with exemplified real servant leadership. Just a few months prior to the US event of 9/11 in 2001, my faith journey started to look to Jesus.

Then in October of 2002, at a Via de Cristo 3-day weekend #42, the reality of my faith transformed. My following Jesus became profound, reinforced, and reinvigorated. It changed my direction. I found my childlike heart once more. A few men and I started meeting weekly to act as a small accountability group.

Soon after that, a retired pastor who attended this weekend with me agreed to be my mentor. Originally, he was a bricklayer, then became a pastor by attending seminary part time. We kept our time open and free to discuss anything. He answered question after question. And he guided me into studying the old testament references restated in the new testament.

In retrospect, he became the grandfather I had lost 10 years prior who was also a builder, a finish carpenter. This feels much more significant now, than it did at the time. Unfortunately, He died just a couple years after he started mentoring me.

Not long after his death, my employer moved his company to Arizona. Susan and I decided we were not in a position to move, so we did not follow. I found myself seeking another job. Within a couple of months, I had three offers.

I went to seek The One True God's will for me. Then, for the first time, I heard Him, I would say even audibly. "Be who I made you to be." I took that as the answer for the operations manager position with the pool company. This job was very challenging, new people, new industry, and I was beginning to show my faith to others at work.

During these few years, I hit my lowest valley since turning toward Jesus. We had been seeking medical help to conceive a child. During that time, we discovered Susan had fibroids in her uterus, which we went to surgery to remove. Before she left, she told me specifically, don't let them take it all away. She knew far more about her family history than I did.

Within 30 minutes of wheeling her away. The surgeon explained it was hopeless, and this was the worst case of fibroids he had ever seen. And that he could stop, or remove, her uterus and end the pain she had been experiencing for several years. I believe selfishly, I said to remove it.

That day broke me. I had to look into her eyes and confess that I took away her option of motherhood. I could not emotionally take this, so I ran away like a child and back to work for a week, leaving her alone with this physical and emotional pain. In retrospect, I was still a child living a man's life. I was so distracted she had to call her sister, two hours away, to pick her up and take her home. Of my regrets, this is in the top three.

I cannot even fathom being that man, but I was. It is His will that we stayed together after my betrayal. Sometime, in the few years following, we both just looked at each other and forgave each other for everything. At least we said it. It took years longer for the relationship to actually reveal it.

And it was not until the completion of this book, did His Spirit reveal to me that I had a root of bitterness from not having children in my flesh. This has affected me and us for too many years of our marriage. He helped me remove it and the wound is now healed. Thank you, Jesus! He is faithful.

Many months after the surgery, I felt Him leading me away from that pool company position. So, opportunities came for me to hire help and prepare for my departure. Within days of them coming on board, an opportunity to build churches again came through my dearest hometown, friend David B., with a division of his employer. I was there a couple of months later.

Later that year, just after an Assemblies of God Leadership Convention, I felt the need for a mentor again. From my relationships within Via de Cristo, I found my second mentor, pastor David H. He is now a dear friend. 15+ years later, we still talk almost every week. We have kept this commitment through several years by meeting in person, then by phone for the nine months while I was in Asia, and now again by phone as I live in Arizona.

During my time with David H, I recall a very specific conversation at breakfast at a Cracker Barrel restaurant, where we discussed the many complexities of scripture. It was that day where a seed by His Spirit was planted. Because The One True God is what He is and scriptures are His Words, we debated they must be accurate with no contradictions, and throughout everything would be interconnected. If it was not, then either His Word was mistranslated, or I misunderstood it.

At that time, I saw many contradictions, thus many more questions. That week, I started to further research human creation vs. evolution. What I discovered was the evidence for creation and scriptures accuracy was far beyond what I was taught.

Seeking

Since that Friday with David H, I have been trying to determine the interconnected Truth of scripture. As a person in the construction industry, I have the mind of a builder. Building to me is just a puzzle in three dimensions.

I build knowledge and understanding like I build any project or building. There are many parts, and each one has a function interconnecting with another. When something does not fit, you must look at all the surrounding components to determine why.

If you consider knowledge and understanding more like a two-dimensional puzzle, each piece fits in both shape and color to its adjacent pieces. Common puzzles have a photo of the finished result to help determine where unique pieces fit. They also have pieces with a smooth edge to help frame the complete puzzle. However, with knowledge and understanding, the puzzle has no clear finished picture, or any defined edges.

One of our greatest challenges with knowledge and understanding is that other people teach you and try to assist with assembling your "puzzle." Your knowledge is influenced by their understanding. Depending on what they know or believe, that influence could help you or hurt you. There are basically four types of teachers: 1. honest and knowledgeable, 2. honest and ignorant or mislead, 3. dishonest and knowledgeable, and 4. dishonest and ignorant or mislead.

Depending on which type of teacher is helping you with the puzzle of knowledge, only the first type of teacher will benefit you. The others could ignorantly or intentionally mislead you. Those teachers have a direct impact on your understanding and faith. This is why knowledge and understanding of The One True God is so challenging to put together. This is why personal research and study are important.

Throughout these years, I listened to many teachers. Many parts of their teachings did not connect. This is when His Spirit led me to read the scriptures for myself and stop just listening to teachers.

Today, to overcome these challenges, I simply ask His Spirit questions. He will lead me into the research to show me more understanding. He always honors my request and does, confirming the deeper and wider interconnected truth of His Word.

Once again in 2009, I found myself looking for work. The economic downturn had all church congregations scared, and no one was building. As always, He was guiding me. After a few months of freelancing, my friend, David B., pointed me to an opportunity. It was back in the commercial swimming pool industry.

By November that year, I was living in Asia to build an iconic infinity edge pool. I was there specifically to lead the local contractor team and our team through construction and the grand opening. Susan was able to join me for the week of Chinese New Year and then fully in April until we returned in July.

My Singaporean friends were very strong Christians, and I started attending and following their TV pastor. In Asia, I studied and started to pray "in tongues." Once back in the US, I realized how controversial this was to many Christian denominations. I felt from those around me it was wrong and stopped.

Then, five years later in fall of 2015, my very close friend, Sean R., and I were driving to a Via de Cristo event and talking of many of our concerns and speaking in tongues came up. As clearly as yesterday, I remember him saying with his upbringing it was natural, and I should continue. I did. What followed was an intense time of prayer, study, and surrendering to His Spirit. I felt an enormous push to know much more and started to sincerely immerse myself in His word, seeking Him.

As Paul clarifies in 1 Corinthians 12- 14, I was "edified" or "built-up" by this these unknown tongues. And the result of this "building up," I discovered I understood scripture with greater clarity and interconnectivity. A recent example was when Paul said, "they heap to themselves teachers." It now made more sense. I understood the subtlety of his words. The way to heap teachers about you is to surround yourselves with their books.

A few months after this push to learn more, I became very frustrated with my working situation. I was prepared to resign from the company. Susan stopped me and said I could leave any time, as long as I had another job ready. She knew the significant drain on my time at work and constant high stress this job was hurting me and us. Again, He had already planned for the move. My friend, from the architect, who help me come back to Jesus, had a position coming open in six weeks.

With this new role, I traveled throughout the state with hours of driving time each week. He prompted me to take this uninterrupted time and learn. For many of those weeks, I was listening to 20 hours or more of Christian teaching from many pastors and evangelists and denominational beliefs.

I found new understanding in these teachings and started to follow some of them. Then the more I learned, again, I discovered I was following false teachings. It is amazing how easily we can be manipulated with just half truths. Susan prompted me to read more within scripture to discern the Truth. His Spirit helped clarify the discrepancies.

Back to the Desert

In June of 2018, Susan and I finally took our first ever, full two-week vacation to celebrate our 25th wedding anniversary. In all our years together, including the two years in college, we had never had two weeks without work or school. It was like breathing for the first time. Days upon days were spent with just each other and the waves of the ocean surrounding Kauai. Our only connection to others was her mobile phone. We kept it active for any family emergencies.

We immersed ourselves in this natural beauty and thought about our ideal location to live. We questioned why we still lived in Indiana and started listing the places we would like to live. We remembered our multiple trips to Arizona and decided that sometime within the next five years we would start moving to Hawaii or the Southwest.

Throughout those two weeks, Susan spoke to my brother many times to provide encouragement and advice. One of the times, a coworker texted her about an upcoming opportunity with an office opening in Scottsdale. A couple of calls later, there was a real possibility of us relocating to Arizona. When we discussed it, I confirmed to her that in the last few years, His Spirit told me to be prepared to move from our home.

Before this week, I presumed we would move near other friends in various cities in the few surrounding states or just to the south side of Indy. No, He knew we had to move from the green of the Midwest to the deserts of Arizona. He was opening the doors ahead of us. He will always prepare you before he will move you.

Later that year, we headed west to start anew in Arizona, truly separating from our family, friends, and our Christian support, and our ministry with Via de Cristo. This ministry and the people became a huge part of our lives before the move. Once we settled in Arizona, it was clear our personal problems followed us.

I did not expect this. I thought starting over in a new environment would mean a fresh start, with a clean slate. What we discovered was that our personal issues and things interfering with our marriage were impossible to ignore without the distractions of others.

During our transition to Arizona, I was already well into this search of spiritual warfare and the "open" doors of demonic influence on our lives. I committed to Susan that we would finally be rid of it all, the junk and dirt of the evil spirits that plagued us from the past. Learning about it and putting it into practice are two completely different things.

In the first year, since that commitment, several things changed with my faith journey. One change was that I started to boldly declare, confess, and repent of our sins and close the "open doors" of our families' generational sin and any potential curses we have gained. For each one, I systematically took the authority of Jesus over our lives and my authority over our household. I closed the doors and removed the curses. It has taken several years and has been one of our greatest challenges.

Another change was that we started to remove and destroy cursed items in our possession. In that first year, He guided me to a crystal I had kept from my vision quest travels. This had been used in various occult practices prior to my returning to Jesus. Yet several decades later, I still had it. Although I had dismissed its relevance, and thought of throwing it into the trash with every new move, I just could not get rid of it.

He instructed me to destroy it. So, with courage and trepidation, I took a hammer and shattered it. Immediately, I felt physically lighter and later discovered my pornography addiction was gone. I found the deeper meaning to the passage below.

Proverbs 26:2 states:

"As the bird by wandering, as the swallow by flying, so the curse causeless shall not come."

Another change was that I went from speaking "in tongues" to singing "in tongues." My joy of speaking just naturally grew to singing. I discovered this was a truly magnificent and natural expression of surrender and my worship. It is never a tune or words I know, but my spirit sings and composing as I go.

My worship with singing in tongues is truly a new song. I found later that Paul describes it in Ephesians 5, 1 Corinthians 14, and Romans 15. In further research, I found references to a "new song" in Isaiah 42, The Revelation 5 & 14, and in Psalms 33, 40, 90, 96, 144, & 149. This has been a constant in my life since then.

With both speaking and singing "in tongues," sometimes there is a specific issue or concern in my mind which I am expecting clarification. Sometimes, it just comes and when I am done, I seek the interpretation of it. Occasionally, there is a specific answer, or a general answer for me or another person. And yet other times the answer is "just wait."

The last major change was that I was invited to join a weekly Tuesday morning "Listening Prayer" in Mesa by a ministry friend of a friend from Indianapolis. I accepted right away. I started with the group in April and thought this time would be like other "weekend reunion" or accountability group I had been in. It was not.

We started very early in the morning and did not eat. We did not talk about our highs and lows of the week. Instead, we gave a three minute "check-in" for any prayers needed and then jumped into 45 minutes praying and seeking scripture in silence. That was new to me. I had never prayed that long before. I believe I checked the time every 10 minutes.

After the 45 minutes of silence, we share with the small group some or all of what we found interesting. This is, of course optional, not everything you are led to is meant to be shared. I remember early in that first year, His Spirit directing me to:

Psalm 5:2-3:

"Hearken unto the voice of my cry, my King, and my God: for unto thee will I pray. My voice shalt thou hear in the morning, O LORD; in the morning will I direct my prayer unto thee, and will look up."

The morning prayer group and this time became a catalyst in my faith journey. I discovered the real power in spending the first part of your day with Him. These Tuesdays, even years later, are just as impactful for me. I need this fresh, morning time away from the noise of a busy day in a busy life. It was this clarity in my life that led me to commit the first hour every day to Him to write this book.

Throughout these first months of Tuesday mornings, I was waiting for His clarity on "What now?" Here we are in Arizona, fighting against all the junk of our past, but why here? He could have easily led me to a similar group and other changes in Indiana. Then, on August 27, 2019, His Spirit led me to commit to 40-day fast.

Before that day, I had only fasted for a few days or series of Fridays. I began to panic at the thought of 40 days with no food. That morning, I kept asking and clarified what this forty-day fast would look like for me. As I was asking, I thought of Abraham negotiating with Him to spare the valley of Sodom and Gomorrah.

When we finished, He agreed that I would have a modified fast with, every evening meal and liquids all day. Also, I would not skip a meal that had an opportunity to have lunch or breakfast, if it helped me with relationships with my wife and my new friends at work. Even with the skipped days for those meals, it still only took 44 days.

Throughout the fast, I prayed and journaled, and found His Spirit was burning within me. On October 10, 2019, I finished. It landed exactly on the Thursday I was to leave for the Tres Dias weekend. When I had completed the forty-day fast, I expected a miracle. But that morning was just like the all the previous mornings.

I confessed my disappointment to Susan that I did not receive any great revelation in His Spirit. And she said what I was waiting for was simple, "serve the elderly... like you do with Via de Cristo." She had plainly said what I was seeking. I received the sprout of a seed he had planted many years before. It was Jubilee Days.

That afternoon, I embarked on my first Tres Dias weekend. Until now, I had only served on Via de Cristo in Indiana and Kentucky, a similar 3-Day weekend. I was serving on the prayer team. In the weeks prior to the event, which coincided with the fast, I prayed for the people serving on the team and being served on the weekend.

On the weekend, I stayed up late with little sleep, counseling and spiritually battling, as He called me. But most of all, I found deep and personal joy in His presence flowing through me. His Spirit kept pointing me to things He wanted for Jubilee Days. As I was led, I shared the vision of Jubilee Days with a few of these new friends. They were ready to help.

Additionally, He confirmed I needed someone within leadership of Kairos, the prison version of the 3-Day weekends. So, trying to be true to His promptings, after the Tres Dias weekend, I made a few calls and ended up talking to Nellie A. Who is now one of Jubilee Days strongest advocates and a dearest friend. If you asked her, she would say she was waiting for this call and Jubilee Days to become a reality.

I was overwhelmed when His Spirit confirmed for me to lead a group through developing a new version of these weekends, specifically for those in care facilities. I had experienced this same feeling from my past career with helping churches build expansions and have fundraising campaigns. I saw many of these groups step out in faith and accomplish something truly beyond their capabilities or foreseeable resources.

I have heard Christians use the expression, "God will never give you more than you can handle." This is usually used in times of difficulty or grief. My experience is different. I find that if it comes from Him, it will always be beyond what you or I can handle. He wants to prove that He can do more than we can imagine. If we surrender to His will, He will make our life greater and more fulfilling than our own understanding.

Just like Jubilee Days was a seed growing, so was 40. After meeting for a few months with the wonderful men and women who helped shape and clarify Jubilee Days, His Spirit led a Saturday morning conversation with David H where The 40 Foundations of Faith© (40 FoF) was mentioned. Once it was said out loud, it was clear that was what He wanted.

His Spirit told me that these 40 FoF would take time to complete. They would be a significant part of this team's work and be more than just the key points for Jubilee Days.

He did not tell me it would take a year of prayer and occasional fasting to even get these 40 FoF sketched out. Then it would take another four (4) years, over sixty meetings, and additional research and the completion of this book to fully vet them. I do not know if my commitment was that strong then. I know now; it was.

When we started in November of 2019, I had believed that Jubilee Days would be ready to start within one year. I saw all the necessary steps and was running on His Spirit's adrenaline. Our meetings were dynamic and confirming. Except, my heart broke every time we hit resistance, with both completing the work of preparation and discussing it with facilities.

In May 2022, we took a break from these meetings. The end of discussions and planning was becoming visible. We had finally worked through all the concepts and operational details of how these events would occur online or in other environments. Additionally, we had just finished the third round of reviewing the 40 Foundations of Faith©. Then in early August, one of our core group, Otto L, died in a hospital.

His death devastated me and cooled my enthusiasm. I grieved for nearly a year. I met him on that first Tres Dias weekend. This was not only the loss of a now very close friend, but a friend who always challenged me about what would be the purpose and message of Jubilee Days. Since those first few days, he kept me assured of its potential future impact. I know in my heart these years of meetings and other discussions strengthened his faith and commitment to Jesus before leaving us.

Just after starting this book, I realized I allowed Otto's death to be a curse on this book and Jubilee Days. I trust Jesus's words that say we have the power to bind and loose on earth and in heaven. This means with His Spirit, we have the power to break and bind the supernatural, which affects our physical world.

I repented of my rebellion of not seeking Him for help and disobedience by delaying this book. I broke that curse. Since that day, I have not stopped giving Him my first hour of every morning. It is the same resolve as I did on the original 40-day fast, only without the fast.

Recently, I watched the animated version of The Pilgrim's Progress. It is an allegory written by a priest in the early 1600s. The same truths of those Christians, then, hold true today. It is a journey, day by day, week by week, year by year. Experiencing His Spirit brings the same joy that King David, Moses, Adam, Eve, the early followers, and Jesus did. Embrace it and enjoy the adventure of not following what this world has, but what your creator, The One True God, has planned for you.

In our journey, we are constantly told we are not of value. However, we are far more important than the world systems tell us. Although Jesus died so that billions of individuals would have a choice, I believe He would have done it just for me and Susan. He did it for one couple in the Garden of Eden, one family on the ark, and one people in the desert.

In the desert, we experience the life-giving effect of water differently. A few gallons of water brings plants to life. A few days of rain will turn the desert green. This can be seen in the flat valleys, depths of the Grand Canyon and rock cliff of buttes. The desert, seemingly lacking any life, is in fact teeming with it, just dormant.

You have the same worth as the people in The Scriptures. You are the tree in the desert waiting for the rain. As stated in John 4, Jesus is the living water. In the midst of all the harshness of our environments, your life will flourish if connected to Him and His living water.

The Finish, but not The End

I have no formal education in divinity. I have been stopped many times by His Spirit and other counsel from pursuing it. Oddly, at a time of substantial change in my life and career, a pastor told me my influence would be greater without being one of them.

Was it another moment of prophecy in my life? At the time, I would not agree. I was frustrated with those ideas. I thought I knew my path. I did, at least, until I stopped rebelling. In that act of acceptance of what and who I am, I found He directed my path clearly, and always within His timing.

Although I have not attended accredited classes, I have spent much of the last many years reading from those leaders and teachers who are deeper in spiritual warfare and scriptural interpretation: Dean Odle, Rebecca Brown, Michael W. Smith, Watchman Nee, Frank & Ida Mae Hammond, Dave Roberson, Ken Johnson, and Derek Prince. I have also listened to and watched various teachers, through the last 20+ years.

However, now when I listen to them or read their books, I ask His Spirit to guide me and give discernment. I do not let others' opinions or teachings become my own until I verify it with Scripture and prayer. I have been massively deceived in my past and suffered through the pain of cognitive dissonance. I do not risk being misled or misleading Susan or others again.

This book, this study, and my personal experiences are here for you. I have asked His Spirit throughout these months of writing to show me what He wants on these pages.

You may have noticed that this study did not directly discuss some of the bigger controversial questions, such as:
- Creation vs evolution
- Cessation of spiritual gifts
- Demonic deliverance
- Eternal spiritual security
- Where our spirit or soul goes when we die
- The rapture
- Acceptable biblical texts.

Additionally, the study did not review:
- Biblical cosmology
- The Creator's calendar
- Giants and extraterrestrials
- The other great flood
- Eschatology
- Non-biblical Christian traditions.

However, many of the scriptural examples within the 40 Foundations of Faith© cover them. And my personal testimony clearly indicates my understandings of many of these.

As Believers and Followers of Jesus, we should question and research all of these within scripture and come to a firm understanding for ourselves and those around us.

Proverbs 25:2 beautifully states:

"It is the glory of God to conceal a thing: but the honor of kings is to search out a matter."

Despite these missing elements, I trust you saw my heart for you. As I noted early in the book, One Via de Cristo serenade Saturday night, we sang the song "Here I am Lord" with the verse "I will hold His people in my heart." He led me to pledge to Him those many years ago to hold His people in my heart. I do. Which is why I committed myself to following and obeying Him.

I trust you will grow in your understanding and increase your faith in Him and His Word. I only ask that you share what you have gained with others. Be bold, believe the Truth within scripture and keep putting on your His Spiritual Armor each day.

I sense The Enemy at work more than ever, both with the completion of this book, start of Jubilee Days and as we come into these ever-changing challenging times. There is political and cultural pressure to abandon the Truth of The Scripture, not only in the USA but throughout the world.

A couple of years ago, I was led to the Greek meaning of "deceived" in Paul's letter to his mentee and church leader, Timothy.

2 Timothy 3:1-13 states:

"This know also, that in the last days perilous times shall come. For men shall be lovers of their own selves, covetous, boasters, proud, blasphemers, disobedient to parents, unthankful, unholy, without natural affection, trucebreakers, false accusers, incontinent, fierce, despisers of those that are good, traitors, heady, high-minded, lovers of pleasures more than lovers of God; Having a form of godliness but denying the power thereof: from such turn away.

"For of this sort are they which creep into houses, and lead captive silly women laden with sins, led away with divers lusts, Ever learning, and never able to come to the knowledge of the truth. Now as Jannes and Jambres withstood Moses, so do these also resist the truth: men of corrupt minds, reprobate concerning the faith. But they shall proceed no further: for their folly shall be manifest unto all men, as theirs also was.

*"But thou hast fully known my doctrine, manner of life, purpose, faith, longsuffering, charity, patience, Persecutions, afflictions, which came unto me at Antioch, at Iconium, at Lystra; what persecutions I endured: but out of them all the Lord delivered me. Yea, and all that will live godly in Christ Jesus shall suffer persecution. But evil men and seducers shall wax worse and worse, **deceiving, and being deceived**."*

The King James word "deceived" means "strong delusion." It's like being hypnotized or under a spell. Here in the USA, this is clear everywhere. Most of us are constantly on our smart phones and/or watching television and movies. News and entertainment occupy the vast majority of our lives. We accept what we are shown without question.

Jubilee Days and serving various 3-Day Weekends for over 20 years has required a great deal of time and commitment. This is second only to my commitment to my wife. Both Susan and I have very demanding full-time roles in our careers. Although these pages are mostly about my key moments in my personal spiritual journey, Susan has been and continues to be the most important person on earth to me.

It takes a great deal of time and focus on one another to keep love and a marriage strong. Together, we serve our friends, family, and coworkers. All of my personal and spiritual growth includes her spurring me and supporting me. Our marriage has grown in depth and strength. It has been redefined and lived as we believe we should, biblically, not as this culture or TV teaches.

Susan and I have withstood financial devastation, job losses, severe personal illnesses, loss of future children, death and grieving of close friends and family, teen suicide, and many great spiritual battles. We are committed to one another, beyond anyone else walking this earth and beyond this worldly existence.

This is because of our commitment to Him, The One True God. He has given us the ability to thrive through it all. I believe her life and our marriage are my greatest witnesses to Jesus. No matter what happens in the future, I will be with Him and beside her. We stand together, one flesh living two lives.

To <u>YOU</u> the Reader:

In all the power and authority of Jesus, I bless you. May His Spirit remove the scales from your eyes. May His Spirit show you the Truth as you continue through your scriptural journey. May Jesus restore you, heal you, and lead you into your Jubilee days.

Embrace these verses:

John 4:24:

"God is a Spirit: and they that worship him must worship him in spirit and in truth."

Daniel 12:3:

"And they that be wise shall shine as the brightness of the firmament; and they that turn many to righteousness as the stars for ever and ever."

Jesus will be here one day, and that day will change everything for all of eternity.

www.ingramcontent.com/pod-product-compliance
Lightning Source LLC
Chambersburg PA
CBHW051422090426
42737CB00014B/2793